100
BEST
RESTAURANTS
OF CANADA

Canada's National
Restaurant Guide
to Fine Dining

★★★★★

WANDERLUST PUBLISHING LTD.

ACKNOWLEDGEMENTS

Many thanks to Ivor Sargent, Jerry Mills and Dick MacKay for their encouragement and input into this project, and to my office staff Dominique Reid, Sylvie Gaudet and Teresa Cappelano. Also to the staff and management at O'Keefe Printing in Montreal and to our very talented photographers across Canada. Particular thanks to my Editor, Donna Mills and my Assistant and Production Manager, Anna Lusterio for their dedication to this book, and to the restaurateurs across the country for their encouragement, co-operation and patience.

PRINTED IN CANADA
ISBN 0-9691312-5-9

CONTENTS

SYMBOLS KEY

 Reservations recommended

 Full bar

 Valet parking

 View

 Romantic

 Jacket & tie requested

 Live entertainment

 Wheelchair access

 Private room available

 Outdoor dining

 Health-conscious menu

VEUVE CLICQUOT
LA GRANDE DAME DE LA CHAMPAGNE

INDEX
ALPHABETICAL LISTING OF RESTAURANTS BY REGION

The Publisher of
100 BEST RESTAURANTS OF CANADA
salutes....

THE CANADIAN NATIONAL CULINARY TEAM
~ 1992 ~

Maurice O'Flynn   Clayton Folkers   Fred Zimmerman   Brian Plunkett

Ernst Dorfler   Yoshi Chubachi   Simon Smotkowicz

...on their achievement of the Gold Medal at the
Frankfurt Culinary Olympics

TAYLOR FLADGATE®
THE ORIGINAL LATE BOTTLED VINTAGE.

NEW CLASSIC EUROPEAN

CHARTWELL

791 WEST GEORGIA STREET
~ Four Seasons Hotel, Upper Lobby Level ~
VANCOUVER, BRITISH COLUMBIA
(604) 689-9333

Regional
Vice-President
& General Manager
RUY PAES-BRAGA

Manager
ANGELO CECCONI
Executive Chef
WOLFGANG VON WIESER

All major credit cards
Open daily for breakfast, lunch and dinner

MENU HIGHLIGHTS

★★★★★

APPETIZERS
HOUSE-SMOKED SALMON
GATEAU, CAPER PEPPERCORN
SAUCE • ROASTED ONION AND
SWEET GARLIC SOUP

MAIN COURSES
AHI TUNA, CARAMELIZED PEARL
ONIONS, APPLES & MODENA
BALSAMIC VINEGAR • ROASTED
FRASER VALLEY DUCK BREAST,
APRICOT SHALLOT BREAD
PUDDING, ESPRESSO SAUCE •
JUNIPER-ROASTED VENISON
PAILLARD, HUNTER'S RAGOUT

DESSERTS
APPLE TART TATIN, PECAN
BOURBON ICE CREAM

"CHARTWELL, IN THE FOUR SEASONS HOTEL, IS widely acknowledged to be the city's best hotel dining room. It may also be the finest restaurant." So says *Gourmet Magazine* (July, 1993). Few would disagree. ❦ Recalling the stately Country Manor for which it was named, a portrait of Churchill's summer home, the original Chartwell, dresses the handsome fireplace. Soft seasons of the English countryside are depicted in oils, and inset as panels in rich oak walls. ❦ Executive Chef, Wolfgang von Wieser, works in concert with accomplished Chartwell Chef, Simon Purvis, to bring Old World traditions and New World innovation together at their tables. Classic European knowledge merges with sparkling Asian, East Indian, and North American influences in the highly-original menus (introduced twice annually). Vegetarian and nutritionally balanced "Alternative Cuisine" dishes are also offered. Desserts are brilliant. ❦ Superb service under the direction of respected Maître d', Angelo Cecconi, radiates easy elegance, refinement, experience. ❦ Sommelier, Michael Robidoux, ably represents the award-winning cellar.

AVERAGE DINNER FOR TWO: $65
Does not include wine, tax and gratuity.

LE CROCODILE

#100 - 909 BURRARD STREET
~ Enter from Smithe Street ~
VANCOUVER, BRITISH COLUMBIA
(604) 669-4298

Proprietor & Chef
MICHEL JACOB

Maître d'
JOHN BLAKELEY

All major credit cards
Dinner Mon. to Sat. • Lunch Mon. to Fri.

MENU HIGHLIGHTS
★★★★★

APPETIZERS
ONION TART ALSATIAN STYLE •
GRILLED QUAIL WITH SPINACH
PESTO & CURLY ENDIVE SALAD

MAIN COURSES
FRESH LEG OF LAMB, ROASTED,
SERVED WITH ONION CONFIT AND
MINTED JUS • GRILLED VENISON
MEDALLIONS SERVED WITH
CHANTERELLE SAUCE • GRILLED
ATLANTIC SCALLOPS WITH BASIL
BUTTER SAUCE, SERVED WITH
BLACK LINGUINE

DESSERT
WHOLE POACHED PEAR WITH
CHOCOLATE MOUSSE AND
RASPBERRY COULIS

LE CROCODILE HUMS WITH HAPPY CONVIVIAL-ity, spontaneous laughter and the spirited energy that only a festive French bistro with great pride in itself can generate. ❦ The refreshing, many-windowed setting is enhanced by the easy hospitality of Maître d' John Blakeley and his intelligent, alert service team. ❦ Unfailing excellence and the serious cooking of soft-spoken Owner/Chef Michel Jacob recently earned Le Crocodile top honours in *Gourmet Magazine* as "Vancouver's favourite French restaurant". ❦ Michel practices the cuisine of his native Alsace with patience for nothing short of perfection. A master saucier, he favours homemade veal stock as a demi-glace base for delicacy and depth. The menu is studded with such sensations as Grilled Venison Medallions with Chanterelle Sauce and Grilled Calf Liver with Spinach Pesto. The savory, warm Alsatian Onion Tart starter has, over 10 years, become a signature of Le Crocodile. Each night, two special appetizers and entrées are offered. ❦ The enlightened, largely French wine list highlights special Bordeaux selections and offers an appealing choice of wines by the glass.

AVERAGE DINNER FOR TWO: $60
Does not include wine, tax and gratuity.

THE FIVE SAILS RESTAURANT

999 CANADA PLACE, SUITE 300
~ The Pan Pacific Hotel ~
VANCOUVER, BRITISH COLUMBIA
(604) 662-8111

All major credit cards
Dinner Monday to Sunday

Manager
GAIL McDOWELL

Executive Chef
ERNST DORFLER

MENU HIGHLIGHTS

★★★★★

APPETIZERS
WARM SALMON GRAVLAKS
CRÊPES • DUNGENESS
CRABMEAT SOUFFLÉ • GRILLED
VEGETABLE AND KING PRAWN
SALAD

MAIN COURSES
ROAST RACK OF LAMB WITH
DIJON MUSTARD CRUST
• THAI-STYLE YELLOW SNAPPER
• POACHED WILD SALMON •
GRILLED ATLANTIC LOBSTER •
MONGOLIAN CHICKEN BREAST

DESSERT
GRAND MARNIER SOUFFLÉ

IT IS FITTING THAT *CANADIAN CULINARY Olympic Team Gold Medal Champion*, Chef Ernst Dorfler, should command the kitchen of such an exquisite room. It whispers elegance. The view of Alaska cruise ships ghosting into Vancouver Harbour is idyllic. Formal service, warmed by a distinguished staff, is silken. Manager Gail McDowell's sensitivity for guests is almost prescient. Underlining Executive Chef Dorfler's culinary genius is a simple philosophy: "not only fancy names, not only your creation, but good too..." Foods are married sublimely, not for colour but for flavours. In the preparation of every dish from the Dungeness Crabmeat Soufflé and Roasted Garlic & Leek Soup appetizers, to Roasted Pheasant, Venison Loin, and classic Filet Mignon entrées, traditional disciplines obtain. "A cook has to understand, to care..." says Dorfler. "You learn the old ways. Later you learn to appreciate them. And why." Boris Yeltsin, President Clinton, and Queen Elizabeth have all been guests at Chef Dorfler's table. The impressive international wine collection presented by Sommelier, Joseph Wong, accents French vintages.

AVERAGE DINNER FOR TWO: $80
Does not include wine, tax and gratuity.

Host & Co-proprietor
MANUEL FERREIRA

Chef
SCOTT KIDD

LE GAVROCHE

1616 ALBERNI STREET
~ Downtown ~
VANCOUVER, BRITISH COLUMBIA
(604) 685-3924

All major credit cards
Dinner Mon. to Sun. • Lunch Mon. to Fri.

MENU HIGHLIGHTS

★★★★★

APPETIZERS
MILLEFEUILLE OF SALMON
AND LEEKS WITH CAVIAR •
RAGOUT OF WILD MUSHROOMS
WITH GOAT'S CHEESE SOUFFLÉ

MAIN COURSES
DUCK MAGRET WITH PORT •
BEEF FILET WITH ROOT
VEGETABLES AND SAUCE
BORDELAISE • RACK OF LAMB
DIJONNAISE • TUNA PAVÉ WITH
SMOKED ONION CONFIT, SAUCE
MATELOTE

DESSERTS
WARM MANGO TART WITH
HONEY ALMOND ICE CREAM

LE GAVROCHE HAS BEEN HONOURED SINCE 1979 as "The Most Romantic Place in Vancouver"; dubbed the "Best Place to Kiss"; recommended for "milestone dates" and distinguished in the *Litt Report* as among Canada's top five Small Restaurants. ❧ This is a place for lovers of food, wine romance. ❧ Set in a gently refurbished, two-storey century house with fireplaces, an upstairs terrace and a view, Le Gavroche is always softly intimate. "Good times, good food, good wine" is the credo, and seasoned partners Jean Luc Bertrand and Manuel Ferreira make it so. ❧ Chef Scott Kidd adds his own intelligent and avant-garde twists to French classic cuisine with such refinements as the use of underutilized marine species (skate, crustaceans, geoduck); sensuous simplistic sauces of the lightest natural stocks (clam milk, tomato waters); and uncommon aromatic herbs. Lamb and Bifteck Tartare are superb. ❧ The inspired wine list ("probably one of the best French collections of older vintages") celebrates grand and petit châteaux. Many exclusives. A generous selection by the glass.

14

AVERAGE DINNER FOR TWO: $70
Does not include wine, tax and gratuity

Executive Chef
TONY KAM

GRAND FORTUNE RESTAURANT

217 - 755 BURRARD STREET
~ Corner Alberni, 2nd floor (above Saitoh Canada) ~
VANCOUVER, BRITISH COLUMBIA
(604) 689-9882

All major credit cards
Dinner & Lunch Monday to Sunday

MENU HIGHLIGHTS

★★★★★

APPETIZERS
PEKING DUCK • SMOKED
SALMON • POACHED LIVE
PRAWN AND STEAMED
GEODUCK

MAIN COURSES
WHOLE ABALONE IN CHICKEN
BROTH • SHARK'S FIN AND
SWALLOW NEST • LOBSTER IN
SZECHUAN SAUCE • CRISPY
SEA BASS WITH CHINESE
GREENS

DESSERTS
ALMOND CREAM SOUP
• MANGO PUDDING

BY MOST ENLIGHTENED ACCOUNTS, FRANCIS Liu's Grand Fortune Restaurant is the foremost Cantonese restaurant in town. Vancouver's great hotels recommend it to their guests and in July 1993, *Gourmet* magazine found it worthy of praise. ❦ The restaurant's great popularity among the Oriental community testifies to its authenticity (Japanese is the menu's first language). The seafood tank, alive with crab, lobsters, prawn and rock cod, is the first clue to the freshness one can expect. Dim Sum is a lunchtime (and Sunday) highlight. Dumplings are world-class. ❦ As well as pigeon, pork, and hot pots, the 12-page dinner menu features shark fin specialties, abalone, and swallow's nest delicacies. ❦ Respected on both sides of the Pacific, Executive Chef Tony Kam has been perfecting his art for 35 years. ❦ Service is superb in the lovely 80-guest dining room with etched glass partitions, sliding panels, slate marble, rosewood, oriental art. Three private dining areas accommodate parties of 14, 24, 50.

AVERAGE DINNER FOR TWO: $50
Does not include wine, tax and gratuity.

IL GIARDINO

1382 HORNBY STREET
~ Downtown ~
VANCOUVER, BRITISH COLUMBIA
(604) 669-2422

Proprietor	Chef
UMBERTO MENGHI	GIANNI PICCHI

All major credit cards
Dinner Mon. to Sat. • Lunch Mon. to Fri.

MENU HIGHLIGHTS

★★★★★

APPETIZERS
BRICK-OVEN ROASTED
WILD MUSHROOMS ALL 'OLIO
D'OLIVA • YELLOW SQUASH
CAPPELLETTI IN A SPOT PRAWN
ROSETTE SAUCE

MAIN COURSES
FILET OF REINDEER IN A
JUNIPER BRANDY SAUCE •
OSSO BUCO MILANESE WITH
SAFFRON RISOTTO

DESSERTS
TIRAMISU • WHITE
CHOCOLATE MOUSSE

UMBERTO MENGHI, BEST-KNOWN RESTAURA-
teur in the West, began his success story in 1967 with his
arrival in Canada from Tuscany. Today he commands four
fine restaurants in Vancouver, three in Whistler, and one
in San Francisco; has authored three cookbooks; and
headlines a television show on the cuisine of his native
Italy. ❦ Il Giardino di Umberto, really his flagship restaurant, is a somewhat informal, people-watching place.
Dinner is fabulous and fun. Folks have a good time, both
inside and in the festive courtyard. Meals are a joyful
lesson in Tuscan authenticity. Waiters sometimes sing. ❦
The environment laughs with the warmth of a Tuscan
country villa. Whitewashed walls; terra cotta; lofty, timbered ceilings; living greenery; and windows with views
of the red-tiled courtyard all lend to the happy illusion. ❦
Guests, usually heaping praise on the consistently excellent regional specialties that emanate from his kitchen,
delight in the occasional parades through the room of
gregarious Chef Gianni Picchi. ❦ Alert service is friendly,
informed, generous.❦ The complete wine list is outstanding, with Tuscan wines well represented.

AVERAGE DINNER FOR TWO: $75
Does not include wine, tax and gratuity.

General Manager
BRENDAN MANN

Executive Chef
DAN ATKINSON

SALMON HOUSE ON THE HILL

2229 FOLKESTONE WAY
~ North Shore, across Lion's Gate Bridge ~
WEST VANCOUVER, BRITISH COLUMBIA
(604) 926-3212

All major credit cards
Dinner Mon. to Sun. • Lunch Mon. to Sat. (Brunch Sun.)

MENU HIGHLIGHTS

★★★★★

APPETIZERS
HOMEMADE SMOKED SALMON •
CRAB & SHRIMP CAKE WITH
STRAWBERRY, GREEN PEPPERCORN
SALSA • ALDER-GRILLED FANNY
BAY OYSTERS WITH TRIO OF
SAUCES • B.C. PRAWNS SAUTÉED
WITH TOMATO, LIME, RED GRAPES,
CHILIES AND PEANUTS

MAIN COURSES
ALDER-GRILLED B.C. SALMON •
WASHINGTON STATE LAMB RACK
WITH BLACKBERRIES AND RED
ZINFANDEL DEMI-GLACE
• B.C. SALMON MARINATED IN
DARK SUGARS, DILL AND SALT
WITH PAPAYA SALSA

THIS UNIQUE, HILLSIDE DINING ROOM'S relaxed ambiance might be likened to that of a fine lodge amid fir trees and totems, with a sensational sea view. The room is rich with the scent of an alderwood fire. Soaring ceilings, natural cedar and Native art dominate the soothing decor. ❦ Pacific Northwest alder-grilled fresh seafood (B.C. salmon, flash-seared Vancouver Island sole, coastal prawns) is the specialty of the house, although it's not unusual to find fans returning for Fraser Valley Chicken, Washington Lamb Rack, New York Steak. ❦ General Manager, Brendan Mann, and Executive Chef, Dan Atkinson, work together enthusiastically, divining twists on the traditional. Original salsas, relishes, sauces and desserts are often inspired, and there is no question of Chef Dan's skill and flexibility on the alder grill. The menu, which changes seasonally, offers a daily "fresh sheet" (grilled pork tenderloin, blackened catfish). ❦ Bar Manager Brent Wolrich's well-balanced, *Wine Spectator* award-winning cellar highlights the respected Northwest Coastal wines. ❦ Clearly, the committed management and staff enjoy their work, each other, and pleasing their guests.

AVERAGE DINNER FOR TWO: $50
Does not include wine, tax and gratuity.

JAPANESE/SEAFOOD

Chef/Proprietor
HIDEKAZU TOJO

Chef
NOBU OCHI

TOJO'S RESTAURANT

202 - 777 WEST BROADWAY
~ 10-minute drive from Downtown ~
VANCOUVER, BRITISH COLUMBIA
(604) 872-8050 • 872-8051

All major credit cards
Dinner Mon. to Sat. • Closed for lunch

MENU HIGHLIGHTS

★★★★★

APPETIZERS

TOJO'S TUNA • GINDARA
(BAKED ALASKAN BLACK COD) •
SPECIAL SEAFOOD SALAD

MAIN COURSES
SUSHI:
TOJO MAKI • RAINBOW ROLL •
GOLDEN ROLL •
GREAT CANADIAN ROLL

TATAKI (GRILLED
TUNA MARINADE) • BAKED
LOBSTER

TAKE THE ELEVATOR TO THE SECOND FLOOR, turn right and enter Tojo's, where everything is "a step above". ❦ Consider the healthful offerings of Master Sushi Chef, Hidekazu Tojo, whose innovative, MSG-free delights, created sometimes on the spot, are trademarks. Not to be overlooked are the Nigiri ("individual sushi") and Sashimi ("special tuna") dishes; and the legendary Rainbow Roll, hailed in *Gourmet Magazine* (July 1993). Seasonal blessings, exclusive to Tojo's, abound: Autumn's Stuffed Arctic Char, Winter's Baked Beef and Apple, Springtime's Cherry Blossom Scallops. ❦ "Omakase" is practiced here for customers who prefer to have a meal custom-designed around their personal tastes and budget. Simply put yourself in Tojo-san's hands. ❦ Appreciate the master's artistry from a seat at the open sushi bar, a comfortable tatami room (with leg wells), an intimate booth, or a table with a glorious mountain-and-skyline view. But wherever you sit, discover his creations: "Food for the eye — and for the soul".

AVERAGE DINNER FOR TWO: $60
Does not include wine, tax and gratuity.

18

SWISS-FRENCH

Proprietor & Manager
ERWIN DOEBELI

THE KITCHEN TEAM

THE WILLIAM TELL

765 BEATTY STREET
~ In the Georgian Court Hotel ~
VANCOUVER, BRITISH COLUMBIA
(604) 688-3504

All major credit cards
Dinner Mon. to Sat. • Lunch Mon. to Fri.

MENU HIGHLIGHTS

★★★★★

APPETIZERS
BUNDNERFLEISCH • SALMON
TARTARE • WILD MUSHROOM
BRIOCHE • PAN-FRIED GOAT
CHEESE

MAIN COURSES
STEAK TARTARE • SWISS
CHEESE FONDUE • RACK OF
LAMB • NEW BRUNSWICK
SCALLOPS • SWEETBREADS

DESSERTS
MERINGUE GLACÉE AU
CHOCOLAT • HOT SOUFFLÉS

ERWIN DOEBELI, FOR 29 YEARS OWNER and consummate host of The William Tell, is celebrating his dining room's heritage with the addition of a "Swiss Sheet" to à la carte and special Theatre menus that already excite the palate. Apart from such renowned signature dishes as Smoked Pheasant Fan, Wild Mushroom Brioche, and Scallopini of Young Veal with Morel Sauce, expect to find traditional Rosti, winter Cheese Fondues, Raclette, Émincé de Veau Zurichois, and Steak Tartare. ❦ Under the caring direction of Executive Chef John Rogers, the respect given food is evinced in consistent excellence, beautifully balanced flavours and textures, and meticulous presentation in the *cloche d'argent* style. The hot dessert soufflés may well be the city's best. ❦ Divided into two richly appointed areas with a separate private dining room, the refined, gracious ambiance exudes a soft, relaxed, Old-World polish. Hospitality is unparalleled. Service is expert, personal and welcoming.❦ Sommelier, Mark Davidson, expertly presides over the distinguished collection of more than 160 international wines.

AVERAGE DINNER FOR TWO: $70
Does not include wine, tax and gratuity.

FRENCH

Chef & Proprietor
PIERRE KOFFEL

Manager
BEVERLY KOFFEL

DEEP COVE CHALET

11190 CHALET ROAD
~ 40-minute drive from Victoria ~
SIDNEY, BRITISH COLUMBIA
(604) 656-3541

All major credit cards
Dinner & Lunch Tuesday to Sunday

MENU HIGHLIGHTS

★★★★★

APPETIZERS
UPSIDE-DOWN CHEESE SOUFFLÉ
• LOBSTER MOUSSE

MAIN COURSES
FILET OF LAMB WITH INDIAN
SPICES • EGGS WITH FOIE GRAS •
FRESH LOCAL GAME • LOCAL
FRESH-CAUGHT SEAFOOD • RACK
OF RABBIT • SWEETBREADS

DESSERTS
DESSERT SOUFFLÉS
• CRÈME BRÛLÉE

THERE IS NOTHING PRETENTIOUS ABOUT Strasbourg-born Owner/Chef Pierre Koffel, *or* his kitchen philosophy, *or* the gloriously relaxed "find" of a restaurant he evolved, aside Saanich Inlet on a glorious 6-acre property wrapped in mountains. ❦ Not one to cater to trends, unconventional Chef Pierre shrugs, offhandedly understating his menu as "some French Cuisine classics some not so classic..." when in fact, "not so classic" translates on the plate as fresh, convincing, original, and often inspired twists on the traditional. Local ingredients mean the freshest of everything. Breads, patés, desserts are made here. Salmon is smoked on the premises. A different fish is featured daily. And few can interpret salads and vegetables as can this Chef. ❦ Pierre's "proper" wine reserve — a virtually world-class collection dating from 1902 and estimated at 18,000 bottles — is astounding. ❦ The warmly-appointed dining room banked by windows brimming with views is warmly overseen by Beverly Koffel, whose personal touch and genuine hospitality add greatly to the Deep Cove Chalet experience. ❦ Locals have been keeping this hideaway a word-of-mouth secret for 23 years.

AVERAGE DINNER FOR TWO: $80
Does not include wine, tax and gratuity.

Maître d'
ROBIN BOURNE

Executive Chef
DAVID HAMMONDS
Restaurant Chef
CANDACE PENROSE

EMPRESS ROOM

721 GOVERNMENT STREET
~ The Empress Hotel ~
VICTORIA, BRITISH COLUMBIA
(604) 384-8111

All major credit cards
Dinner Monday to Sunday

MENU HIGHLIGHTS

★★★★★

APPETIZERS
HOUSE-CURED SALMON
• TOURTE OF ESCARGOT •
SMOKED BREAST OF MUSCOVY
DUCK • SHAVED PROSCIUTTO
WITH SUMMER FIGS • ISLAND
DUNGENESS CRAB CAKES •
RAVIOLI OF SWEET POTATO AND
FOREST MUSHROOMS

MAIN COURSES
ROAST GUINEA FOWL • ARCTIC
CHAR WITH LOCAL SPOTTED
PRAWNS • ROASTED PACIFIC
SALMON • LOIN OF LAMB •
FILLET OF BEEF TENDERLOIN WITH
GORGONZOLA RAVIOLI •
METCHOSIN RABBIT SADDLE

APPROACHING VICTORIA HARBOUR, YOU WILL see the Empress Hotel, a grand, regal dowager whose most exquisite jewel is the lovingly-restored, 85-year-old Empress Dining Room. Here, relaxed formality reigns. ❦ Walls rise to 20-foot intricately carved ceilings. Crystal chandeliers and splendid oaken tables shimmer with fireplace light while delicate harp music suspends the grace of Victorian days. ❦ The culinary craftsmanship of Executive Chef David Hammonds and Empress Room Chef, Candace Penrose, is celebrated in their creative, seasonal menus showcasing specialties indigenous to B.C.'s Pacific Coast. Three Mushroom Consommé and Baked Chèvre Tart with Olive and Eggplant are among the inspiring starters. Boneless Quail, Roast Pork Tenderloin, and Pan Fried Local Sooke Trout with Scallops and Gooseberry Compôte are classic entrées. ❦ Pastry Chef Don Nelson's peerless desserts number over 125 different offerings annually. ❦ Faultless service is performed under the direction of respected Maître d', Robin Bourne, the authority on the splendid 350-bottle wine cellar.

AVERAGE DINNER FOR TWO: $80
Does not include wine, tax and gratuity.

FRESH B.C. SEAFOOD

PHOTOS: SIMON DES ROCHERS

Co-proprietor
FREDRICA PHILIP

Co-proprietor
SINCLAIR PHILIP

SOOKE HARBOUR HOUSE

1528 WHIFFEN SPIT ROAD, R.R. #4
~ 40-minute drive from Victoria ~
SOOKE, BRITISH COLUMBIA
(604) 642-3421

All major credit cards
Dinner Monday to Sunday

MENU HIGHLIGHTS

★★★★★

THE SOOKE HARBOUR HOUSE COUNTRY INN FOCUSES PRIMARILY ON LOCAL SHELLFISH AND FISH. THE RESTAURANT USES ONLY FRESH, ORGANIC INGREDIENTS WHICH ARE GROWN IN THE INN'S GARDENS, ON NEARBY ORGANIC FARMS OR HARVESTED IN THE WILD FROM AROUND SOOKE. THE SOOKE HARBOUR HOUSE MENU CHANGES DAILY TO REFLECT THE BEST INGREDIENTS AVAILABLE EACH DAY OF THE YEAR. SALMON, BLACK COD, ROCKFISH, GEODUCK CLAM, ABALONE, CRABS, SEA URCHIN & SHRIMP AS WELL AS LAMB, RABBIT, VEAL, SUCKLING KID & A VARIETY OF VEGETARIAN DISHES FIND THEIR WAY ONTO THE MENU THROUGHOUT THE YEAR.

RIGHT ON THE STRAIT OF JUAN DE FUCA, Fredrica and Sinclair Philip's superb 13-room seaside Inn is an aesthetic, horticultural, marine-biological, culinary marvel. ❦ Sweeping grounds landscaped almost entirely with herbs, edible flowers, berries, fruits and vegetables, roll to the water's edge where, likely as not, you'll find scuba-diving co-owner, Sinclair, harvesting unusual seafood (skate wings, octopus, limpets, or maybe sea urchin) for the next meal (menus change every day of the year). ❦ Sea asparagus grows on the nearby land spit. Lamb, duck, chicken, rabbit come fresh from neighbouring farms. Original taste sensations (Day-Lily Bud Tempura) are yielded by the flower gardens. The chefs can be found foraging in the woods for wild mushrooms and berries. ❦ The cellar features one of Canada's best selection of the finest wines vinted across the country. ❦ *Vogue, The New York Times, Esquire, The Toronto Star, Gourmet, Bon Appetit* and *Le Chef* (Paris) among others have all tried to capture the unique essence of dining in this one-of-a-kind retreat.

AVERAGE DINNER FOR TWO: $75
Does not include wine, tax and gratuity.

ITALIAN

IL CAMINETTO

4242 VILLAGE STROLL
~ Whistler Village ~
WHISTLER, BRITISH COLUMBIA
(604) 932-4442

Proprietor
UMBERTO MENGHI

Chef
MICHAEL LAMPPU

All major credit cards
Dinner 7 days (closed Tues. Oct. - Nov.)
Lunch (Summer: Sat., Sun. & Holiday Mondays)

MENU HIGHLIGHTS
★★★★★

APPETIZERS
B.C. PRAWNS WITH LEMON, TOMATOES & CAPER SAUCE
• ASPARAGUS & SCALLOPS

MAIN COURSES
VEAL SCALLOPINI IN A LEMON PARSLEY SAUCE • TAGLIOLINI PASTA WITH CHICKEN BREAST, LEMON & THYME

DESSERTS
BRÛLÉE WITH FRESH BERRIES
• BLACKCOMB MOUNTAIN SPECIAL

IL CAMINETTO, WHISTLER'S PRE-EMINENT Italian restaurant since its 1981 debut, remains king of the mountain despite the area's proliferation to some 50 dining rooms and cafés. Small wonder. Il Caminetto is the work of mastermind restaurateur, Umberto Menghi (*see Il Giardino, Vancouver*). ❦ Set in the heart of the Village, Il Caminetto is where to "see and be seen". The restaurant happily accommodates 140 in a room that exudes the big-hearted warmth and hospitality of Northern Tuscany. People come for the consistently fine authentic Tuscan cuisine, the fun, and often to encourage romance. ❦ Central in the cozy dining room (rich with colour, bright tilework and lots to entertain the eye) is a grand piano. ❦ The loyal, long-tenure service team, as informed about Whistler as it is about the bountiful menu, is smartly turned out in black and white. A sense of fun shows through in friendly attitudes and cartoon ties. ❦ The choice of international wines is excellent, the emphasis Italian. ❦ "Resort casual" comfortably satisfies the dress code. Delightful summer patio. Candlelit winter evenings.

AVERAGE DINNER FOR TWO: $60
Does not include wine, tax and gratuity.

FRENCH CONTINENTAL

LE BEAUJOLAIS

212 BUFFALO STREET
~ Corner Banff Avenue ~
BANFF, ALBERTA
(403) 762-2712

Proprietors
ESTHER & ALBERT
MOSER

Maître d'
CLAUDE PRAJOUX

All major credit cards
Dinner Monday to Sunday

MENU HIGHLIGHTS

★★★★★

APPETIZERS
HOME-SMOKED B.C. SALMON
ADORNED WITH FRESH CREAM,
CHIVES AND SALMON CAVIAR •
CHILLED CHARCOAL-ROASTED
VEAL LOIN IN PEPPER CRUST
THINLY SLICED WITH TUNA
SABAYON

MAIN COURSES
ROASTED SADDLE OF LAMB AU
JUS WITH PROVENÇAL HERBS
• MEDALLIONS OF BEEF
TENDERLOIN WITH PEPPERCORNS
• ALBERTA FILET MIGNON WITH
SHALLOTS IN RED WINE

WHEN THE CROWN PRINCE OF JAPAN WAS IN Banff, he, like Bob Hope, chose to dine at Le Beaujolais, a lustrous, many-windowed, second-floor hideaway cozied in the embrace of the romantic Canadian Rockies. ❦ True to its splendid reputation as one of Western Canada's finest dining rooms (and Banff's only 1993 *CAA Four Diamond Award* winner), culinary excellence and informal elegance prevail in the best European tradition. ❦ In addition to a popular à la carte menu (showcasing house classics garnered over 13 years), and two 3-course *prix-fixé* menus, a third table d'hôte is offered featuring a superb 6-course "surprise" feast. ❦ Maître d', Claude Prajoux, offers wine selections representative of 5 different grape varieties from select regions around the world. Grand crus, vintages and 12-year-old classics enhance the extensive, expertly-chosen wine list. ❦ Service, of course, is impeccable. ❦ Six languages are spoken. ❦ Dinners only, from 6:00 p.m. ❦ *Associated with Le Beaujolais and also recommended is The Bistro (corner Wolf and Bear Streets). Informal, snug and personal. International menu noon to midnight.*

24

AVERAGE DINNER FOR TWO: $75
Does not include wine, tax and gratuity.

STEAKHOUSE

Proprietors

CON GIANNOULIS · NICK KAKETSIS · LOUIS TSAPRAILIS

CAESAR'S STEAKHOUSE

512 - 4TH AVENUE S.W.
~ Downtown ~
CALGARY, ALBERTA
(403) 264-1222

All major credit cards
Dinner Mon. to Sat. • Lunch Mon. to Fri.

"MORE OIL DEALS HAVE BEEN CUT HERE THAN anywhere else in the West," agree partners Con Giannoulis, Louis Tsaprailis and Nick Kaketsis of their posh 75-seat lounge, 'home to their famous Bloody Caesars'. ❦ This is Caesar's where, for over two decades, high profile visitors and in-the-know Calgarians have been satisfying hankerings for aged, charbroiled, red-brand prime Alberta beef and where second generations come asking for "my father's table". ❦ Four rooms on two levels marry a Roman/Greek theme to seasoned burgundy leather, gleaming brass, rich woodwork and seating for over 200. The centerpiece is Caesar's replica Olympic Torch upon which millions of select rib-eyes, strips, T-bones, filets, racks of spring lamb and lobsters have been fired to perfection over charcoal flame. ❦ The Chef, many of the elite service staff, and (with only minor exceptions) the menu have remained constant since 1972. The consistent quality, personal service and mammoth portions that made Caesar's a word-of-mouth hit can still be depended upon. ❦ Wine list features 70 international choices, some by the glass or carafe. ❦ *A second location, modelled after the original at 10816 Macleod Trail South (403) 278-3930.*

25

AVERAGE DINNER FOR TWO: $65
Does not include wine, tax and gratuity.

Proprietor & Chef
FRANCO COSENTINO

Partner & Chef
MARINO COLONNA

LA DOLCE VITA

916 - 1st Ave. N.E.
~ Little Italy - Bridgeland ~
CALGARY, ALBERTA
(403) 263-3445 • 237-8866

All major credit cards
Dinner Mon. to Sat. • Lunch Mon. to Fri.

MENU HIGHLIGHTS

★★★★★

APPETIZERS
MELENZANA (EGGPLANT) AL
CAPRICCIO • CARPACCIO

MAIN COURSES
AGNELLO MARINATO CON
GRAPPA (LAMB MARINATED IN
GRAPPA) • VITELLO
SCALLOPINE MONTANARA
(VEAL MONTANARA)
• GUINEA FOWL AL
CARTOCCIO

DESSERT
TIRAMISU

FRANCO COSENTINO, HAPPY OWNER/CHEF O
this gem known to most serious diners west of the Prairie
seems everywhere at once. Watching from the kitchen fo
arriving guests, he welcomes you at the door, visits you
table, whips up special surprises, and wishes you a hear
felt good night. His hospitality is genuine. He's a roman
tic. A poet. The consummate host. Since age 12 he ha
practiced culinary art: first at the knee of his grandfathe
then in Torino, Tuscany, Genoa, Paris and Capri. And, a
every guest in the lighthearted, tastefully refreshing 65
seat dining room will testify, he's mastered it. ❦ Soft, ligh
sauces grace superb homemade-today pastas. Regular
travel for miles for Franco's unique Penne Arrabiata; hi
signature homemade Wild Boar Sausage; Pan-frie
Bocconcini Cheese; Grilled Salmon with Shrimp; vea
lamb and game. ❦ A personable, long-tenure team pace
service knowledgeably, expertly.❦ A list of predomi
nantly Italian wines has been carefully chosen to comple
ment the menu. ❦ For a private party of 12 or 14, conside
La Dolce Vita's enchanting, fireplaced, downstairs Lati
Room.

AVERAGE DINNER FOR TWO: $6
Does not include wine, tax and gratuity

Manager of Operations
DARYL RADOMSKY

Proprietor
CARL RADOMSKY

THE INN ON LAKE BONAVISTA

747 LAKE BONAVISTA DRIVE S.E.
~ Southeast Calgary, Lake District ~
CALGARY, ALBERTA
(403) 271-6711

All major credit cards
Dinner Mon. to Sun. • Lunch Mon. to Fri. (Brunch Sun.)

MENU HIGHLIGHTS

★★★★★

APPETIZERS
BALLONTINES OF QUAIL
• DUCK RAVIOLI • ALASKA
KING CRAB CAKES

MAIN COURSES
ROASTED RACK OF LAMB
• ROASTED QUAIL •
CHATEAUBRIAND • SAUTÉED
FROGS' LEGS • DOVER SOLE
VERMOUTH • FILET MIGNON
ROSSINI • FILET OF CHICKEN
& SHRIMP

DESSERTS
INN'S OWN CHEESECAKE
• INN-MADE TIRAMISU • CRÊPES
SUZETTE

THIS UNIQUE PEARL, RESTING ASIDE A SERENE, private 52-acre lake just 15 minutes from downtown, surpasses all expectations of genteel dining in a refined setting. With glass walls and commanding views on three sides, the gracefully appointed Crystal and Newport Dining Rooms brim with natural light during lunch and Sunday Brunch. At dinner, they're pure romance. ❦ Carl and Eunice Radomsky and son Daryl, have, for 16 years, been delighting patrons with their own uncompromising ideas of excellence. Today, the mood is elegantly relaxed and convivial; the service, ingratiating and polished; the international wine list splendid, with 95 careful selections. ❦ The Inn's appealingly eclectic dinner menu shines with creative Californian and Southwestern twists on the classics, such as Cassolette of French Escargot, Duck Salad, Roasted Quail with Morel, Truffle and Madeira Sauce, saddle of rabbit, fresh salmon, grilled Alberta beef, roasted rack of lamb and special light dishes. Desserts are sinful. ❦ Don't overlook the refreshing lakeside terrace and "sea-level" Showboat Bar & Lounge with live entertainment and dancing.

AVERAGE DINNER FOR TWO: $60
Does not include wine, tax and gratuity.

Co-proprietor
ERIC WAH

Co-proprietor
MELVIN SANDERS

THE KING AND I

822 - 11 AVE. S.W., CALGARY, ALBERTA
(403) 264-7241

~ AND ~

10160 - 82ND AVE., EDMONTON, ALBERTA
~ Old Strathcona ~
(403) 433-2222

All major credit cards
Dinner Mon. to Sun. (Calgary), Mon. to Sat. (Edmonton)
Lunch Mon. to Fri.

MENU HIGHLIGHTS

★★★★★

APPETIZERS
THAI-STYLE CALAMARI
(TENDER CALAMARI WITH
GINGER CHILI SAUCE) • BASIL
SCALLOPS (BAKED WITH
FRESH BASIL AND CHILI JAM)

MAIN COURSES
CHU CHU KAI
(CHICKEN TENDERLOINS
STIR-FRIED WITH ORIENTAL
VEGETABLES IN AN OYSTER
CHILI SAUCE) • NUEA PAD
PRIG (MARINATED BEEF
SAUTÉED WITH WILD
MUSHROOMS AND HOMEMADE
CHILI SAUCE)

PARTNERS ERIC WAH, MEL SANDERS AND HOA Chung were, in 1988, the first to bring Thai cuisine to Calgary. Within six months, patrons "lined up on the street". Inside a year, the original The King and I expanded by two-thirds and, in '91, the new Edmonton location launched a second triumph. ❦ In Calgary, it's big, bold and jazzy with dropped ceilings, breezy contemporary decor and seating for nearly 200. In Edmonton, it's a lively, funky, off-the-beaten-track, 50-chair, come-as-you-are favourite in the eclectic Old Strathcona district. ❦ Happily, in both locations the 64-item MSG-free menu (with many vegetarian dishes) is identical, and so is the outstanding quality, authenticity and considerate service. ❦ Both kitchens are run by members of the Chung family (former proprietors of one of old Saigon's best restaurants) and only the finest ingredients go into the memorable satays, curries, chicken, seafood and pork dishes. Perfect sauces are all homemade. Basil scallops, spring rolls, prawns, Thai-style calamari, and chicken tenderloin dishes are all standouts. ❦ Wines by the glass, litre or half-litre; or from a popular international list.

AVERAGE DINNER FOR TWO: $38
Does not include wine, tax and gratuity.

PHOTOS: DANIEL RANDON

Manager
BRIAN WELSH

Executive Chef
BRIAN GREEN

THE CARVERY
OF EDMONTON

10135 - 100 STREET
~ Westin Hotel ~
EDMONTON, ALBERTA
(403) 493-8994

All major credit cards
Dinner Mon. to Sun. • Lunch Mon. to Fri. (Brunch Sun.)

"NO ONE EVER LEAVES HUNGRY..." SMILES Executive Chef Brian Green. But then, why should they when The Carvery menu boasts an expertly prepared roast double breast of chicken, buffalo tenderloin, 14-ounce surf and turf, rack of lamb, venison, and 16-ounce Dover sole. ❦ For 17 years The Carvery has been presenting regional favourites...Western comfort cuisine...in a fine dining atmosphere. Timbered Tudor styling dominates the handsome room that sparkles with crystal, silver and crisp white linen. Ethereal harp music floats through the room as guests relax in cozy armchairs. Seasoned professionals are there to pamper. ❦ From the Chef's paté, special breads and flavoured butters, to The Carvery's Signature Cake and liqueur trolley, everything is flavoured with excellence. Special imports and vintages grace the 130-bottle wine list which offers many selections by the glass or half-bottle. ❦ Although recognized as a Distinguished Restaurant of North America (DIRONA); as a 1993 *CAA Four Diamond Award* winner; and as one of Canada's "Top 10," an honour bestowed by *EnRoute*, The Carvery is not content to rest on its laurels.

AVERAGE DINNER FOR TWO: $70
Does not include wine, tax and gratuity.

PACIFIC RIM/CALIFORNIA

Proprietor & Chef
PETER LAI

Maître d'
THOMAS BAUMANN

THE CHEF'S TABLE

11121 - 156 STREET
EDMONTON, ALBERTA
(403) 453-3532

All major credit cards
Dinner Mon. to Sun. • Lunch Mon. to Fri.

MENU HIGHLIGHTS

★★★★★

APPETIZERS
GRAVLAKS, CUCUMBER
VINAIGRETTE, FIELD GREENS
• GRILLED POLENTA, WILD
MUSHROOMS, HERB WINE
CREAM SAUCE GRATINEÉD
WITH THREE CHEESES

MAIN COURSES
GRILLED DOUBLE BREAST OF
QUAIL, GARLIC SHALLOT
COMPOTE • GULF SHRIMP
WITH PROSCIUTTO, BASIL,
GOAT CHEESE CREAM SAUCE
• ROASTED BONELESS RABBIT
WRAPPED IN PANCETTA
VEGETABLE FLAN

"TO SAY YOU HAVE NEVER HEARD OF PETER Lai or The Chef's Table is as if to say you have never seen your own feet" said one local review. Lai's restaurant "stacks up against the best in San Francisco and New York...innovative...current...I'd take anyone there" says Maurice O'Flynn, manager of Team Canada's gold-medal Culinary Olympic Squad. With more than a dash of adventure, Owner/Chef Peter Lai demonstrates his understanding of the nature of flavours and the freshness of modern cuisine in perfectly balanced creations inspired by the classics. Homemade Cajun-spiced Chicken Sausage, Curry Snail Soup, Grilled Deep-Sea Scallops with Thai Sauce and Coconut Rice; Sole Rolled with Asparagus, Shitake Mushroom and Lobster Roe are examples. Hailed by food critics as one of Canada's finest California cuisine restaurants, The Chef's Table satisfies a powerful, devoted clientele with its serene environment softly veiled in shades of pink, grey and rose; expert service; and outstanding fare complemented by a sophisticated list of wines of the world. Don't let the unassuming mall location fool you.

AVERAGE DINNER FOR TWO: $50
Does not include wine, tax and gratuity.

FRENCH CONTINENTAL

General Manager
CLAUDE BUZON

Chef
SONNY DAO

CLAUDE'S ON THE RIVER

9797 JASPER AVENUE
~ In the Edmonton Convention Centre ~
EDMONTON, ALBERTA
(403) 429-2900

All major credit cards
Dinner Mon. to Sat. • Lunch Mon. to Fri.

MENU HIGHLIGHTS

★★★★★

APPETIZERS
WILD MUSHROOM SOUP •
FROGS' LEGS • ESCARGOT
MONTE CRISTO (CLAUDE'S
OWN)

MAIN COURSES
RACK OF LAMB • ALBERTA
BEEF TENDERLOIN • FRESH
SEAFOOD • RAGOÛT DE
FRUITS DE MER • SALMON

DESSERTS
ASSORTMENT OF CLASSICS

THE NAME OF THE EARLIER RESTAURANT, Claude's On 107th Street, still falls trippingly from the lips of many Westerners describing their finest dining experiences. Now the new place overlooking the Saskatchewan River shines as 'Claude's' personal best. ❦ With spacious accommodation for 120, four softly sensuous rooms bloom with graceful, romantic sophistication. Creamy linen, comforting pastels and panoramic views dominate the tranquil decor, while a distinguished service staff faultlessly attends guests under the direction of Claude himself. ❦ Chef Sonny Dao performs kitchen magic on wild Nova Scotia salmon, Australian spring lamb, milk-fed veal, pheasant, fowl, pork, and Alberta beef. Desserts are indulgent. À la carte and a 5-course table d'hôte menus are offered, special requests are welcomed. ❦ Gracing the stellar wine list are nearly 100 thoughtfully described selections from around the world, including rare and fine vintages.

AVERAGE DINNER FOR TWO: $70
Does not include wine, tax and gratuity.

Manager	Executive Chef
LEANNE PAWL-SMOLIAK	WILLIE WHITE

THE HARVEST ROOM

10065 - 100TH STREET
~ Hotel Macdonald ~
Canadian Pacific Hotels & Resorts
EDMONTON, ALBERTA
(403) 424-5181

All major credit cards
Dinner and Lunch Monday to Sunday

MENU HIGHLIGHTS

★★★★★

APPETIZERS
CREAM OF WILD MUSHROOM &
ARTICHOKE SOUP • ORANGE
AND TARRAGON RAVIOLI WITH
ESCARGOTS & OYSTER
MUSHROOMS

MAIN COURSES
LAMB LOIN BRUSHED WITH
ROSEMARY & DIJON PASTE ON
A BLACK CURRANT SAUCE •
ROAST VEAL CHOP WITH
SAFFRON & PIMENTO SAUCE ON
PEPPER FETTUCINI

DESSERTS
GOLDEN CREAM CHARLOTTE
WITH APRICOT GLAZE SPONGE,
GALLIANO & BING CHERRIES

WARMTH AND SIMPLE OPULENCE EXUDE FRO the lovingly refurbished Harvest Room, an enchantir Edmonton tradition wherein grand windows with soot ing views soar to vaulting, chandeliered ceilings; a reg stone terrace lords over the river valley; and the "bistr ish" simplicity of an open kitchen underline the unimposir elegance of the intimate room. ❦ Chef Willie White splendid dinner menu sports a gold medal from t *Alberta Hotel Association*, naming it among the best '93. Five tempting appetizers, four salads and such inv ing soups as Cream of Wild Mushroom and Artichoke; "Southwest" White Bean, Tomato and Spicy Sausag lead off the choices. Charbroiled swordfish, B.C. salmo Alberta beef, and unique Harvest Room veal, lamb, ar chicken specialties are featured. A vegetarian cuisine also available. The Chocolate Marquis on Espresso Bea Sauce dessert is peerless. ❦ Black tie service is discreet attentive and relaxed. ❦ Fine wines from around the wor and a Private Reserve list dominate the cellar. An exce lent selection is available by the glass.

AVERAGE DINNER FOR TWO: $
Does not include wine, tax and gratui

General Manager
JIM GORDA

Manager
ELAINE REICHELT

THE VINTAGE ROOM

10235 - 101 STREET
~ Edmonton Hilton ~
EDMONTON, ALBERTA
(403) 428-7111

All major credit cards
Dinner Tuesday to Saturday

MENU HIGHLIGHTS

★★★★★

APPETIZERS
MARINATED ATLANTIC SALMON
TARTAR, CRISP POTATO WAFERS
& SWEET MUSTARD SAUCE •
GLAZED DUNGENESS CRABMEAT
• BROILED QUAIL WITH SMOKED
BACON ON FIELD GREENS &
SHALLOT VINAIGRETTE

MAIN COURSES
SAUTÉED TOURNEDO OF BEEF
WITH GOOSE LIVER • ROAST
BREAST OF DUCK WITH RED
ONION CONFIT, CRANBERRY WINE
SAUCE • STEAMED MEDALLIONS
OF MONKFISH, SAUTÉED
SPAGHETTI SQUASH & MUSTARD
SEED SAUCE

NEWLY REOPENED AFTER A TWO-YEAR refinement, the distinguished Vintage Room's original elegance has evolved into a relaxed, polished sophistication. ❦ Richly panelled and mirrored walls, crystal chandeliers, soothing music, candlelight, buttery leather armchairs, and immaculate table settings comprise a comfortable, warm atmosphere for just 60 guests aptly attended by Manager, Elaine Reichelt, and her team. ❦ Traditional classics with a lighthearted flair command the menu. Order à la carte, or choose innovative dinner recommendations which change weekly. ❦ Amicable waiters perform with style and pride. ❦ Great care has been taken to create an expansive and reasonable wine list that enhances the cuisine. A selection by the glass is offered.

AVERAGE DINNER FOR TWO: $60
Does not include wine, tax and gratuity.

REGIONAL CANADIAN

Maître d'
GUY VALLEE

Chef
DAVID MACGILLIVRAY

EDITH CAVELL DINING ROOM

~ Jasper Park Lodge ~
JASPER, ALBERTA
(403) 852-3301

All major credit cards
Dinner Monday to Sunday

MENU HIGHLIGHTS

★★★★★

APPETIZERS
CHOWDER OF FIELD & FOREST
MUSHROOMS WITH PRAIRIE GRAINS
& FIREWEED HONEY

MAIN COURSES
COLLUPS OF BEEF MUSKOX LOIN,
VENISON SAUSAGE, HUCKLEBERRY
RELISH & ARCTIC BERRY JUS
LIÉGOISE • RATATOUILLE FLAN
WITH OKA CHEESE, CHIVE
CUSTARD & SUN-DRIED TOMATO
CREAM

DESSERT
OATMEAL CINNAMON SHORTCAKE
WITH WARM PEACH MACÉDOINE &
DEVON CREAM

SET IN ONE OF CANADA'S MOST FAMOUS AND spectacular lodges, the elaborate views from the prestigious Edith Cavell Dining Room overlooking Lake Beauvert in the Rocky Mountains will take your breath away. Enter through the Lodge's posh piano bar if you like. ❦ Drifts of white linen and silver warmed by rich cherry oak panelling sweep through four elegant dining areas which, in total, accommodate one hundred guests. ❦ As befits a *CAA Four Diamond Award*-winning resturant, service is discreet and attentive, presentation is glossy. ❦ Believing that "food shouldn't be intimidating, it should be fun" Chef David MacGillivray's culinary style based on heritage home cooking, Alberta ingredients, and creative imagination, has evolved such masterpieces as Cambazola and Morels; Medallions of Grain-Fed Beef Tenderloin with Sauce of Armagnac; and Grilled Alberta Lamb Sausage with Mint Julep Sauce and Raison Pear Chutney. ❦ A remarkable selection of wines represents nearly every important region of the world. Some specialty wines from the cellar are available by the glass.

AVERAGE DINNER FOR TWO: $100
Does not include wine, tax and gratuity.

Executive Chef
BRUNO WUEST

Dining Room Manager
DAN DESANTIS

CORTLANDT HALL
DINING ROOM

2125 VICTORIA AVE.
~ Hotel Saskatchewan Radisson Plaza ~
REGINA, SASKATCHEWAN
(306) 522-7691

All major credit cards
Dinner 6 days (Buffet Sun.) • Lunch 6 days (Brunch Sun.)

MENU HIGHLIGHTS

★★★★★

APPETIZERS
BOUILLABAISE • LOBSTER
BISQUE • PRAIRIE SOUP

MAIN COURSES
SHRIMP IN LOVE
• RACK OF LAMB
• CHATEAUBRIAND
• SALMON EN PAPILLOTTE •
VEAL SWEETBREAD
• VOL-AU-VENT
• CHICKEN LIVER
BROCHETTE

THE TWENTY MILLION DOLLAR RESTORATION is complete. The regal old railway hotel is radiant beyond even its original splendour; and in the grand Cortlandt Hall Dining Room, up to 160 guests are welcomed into a distinctly traditional world of elegant refinement. ❦ Richly appointed in shades of green and burgundy with magnificent crystal chandeliers, French doors and damask napery, Cortlandt Hall, attracting locals and visiting celebrity alike, recalls an era past when dining was an event. ❦ Swiss-born Chef Bruno Wuest's tempting yet uncomplicated menus present quality in quantity for both light and substantial appetites. Shrimp in Love, Rack of Lamb and fresh fish dishes are perennial favourites. Saskatchewan wild rice and Saskatoon berries are used to fine advantage. ❦ Breakfast, lunch, afternoon tea and dinner are offered at Cortlandt Hall with professional, attentive service considerately paced to the time of day. ❦ The well-thought-out wine list features a spectrum of white and red wines from around the world, with an available selection of half-bottles.

AVERAGE DINNER FOR TWO: $70
Does not include wine, tax and gratuity.

FRENCH/SWISS

LE PARISIEN

Proprietor & Chef
ERNEST BOEHME
Chef
PATRICK BOEHME

Proprietor & Hostess
ROSEMARIE BOEHME

106 FRONT ST.
~ 1 hour east of Regina, on Trans-Can. Hwy. ~
WOLSELEY, SASKATCHEWAN
(306) 698-2801

All major credit cards
Dinner Tuesday to Sunday

MENU HIGHLIGHTS

★★★★★

APPETIZERS
DICED SWEETBREADS &
MUSHROOMS • FROGS' LEGS

MAIN COURSES
FILET MIGNON AUX MORILLES •
VEAL SCHNITZEL SIMMERED IN
CREAM & WINE •
BONELESS PHEASANT IN
CHAMPAGNE SAUCE • ELK
STEAK & MUSHROOMS • BEEF
TENDERLOIN SERVED FLAMBÉED
ON A STEEL BLOCK

DESSERT
SOUFFLÉ GRAND MARNIER

MAKE A RESERVATION, THEN HUNT DOWN L
Parisien, the enchanting yesteryear dining room that
making Wolseley (pop. 900) famous. ❦ Arriving in th
1980s with Swiss restaurant experience, owners Erne
and Rosemarie Boehme first set to work hand-restorin
and antique-furnishing two classic turn-of-the-centur
Victorian houses. Today, side-by-side, they house th
family's nostalgic *Banbury House Inn* (a B&B); a locall
popular lounge; and exquisite little Le Parisien, "one c
the finest restaurants between Toronto and Vancouver
❦ Chef Patrick Boehme shares culinary secrets with hi
Chef father, Ernest, while Rosemarie personally hosts th
guests of Le Parisien's two romantic, intimate dinin
rooms. ❦ Outstanding 4-course dinners feature, amon
other indulgences, pheasant, elk steak, frogs' leg:
chateaubriand, fondue, and occasionally bison and wil
boar. The Swiss-inspired *La Portence* (beef tenderloi
flambéd on a steel block) is a house knockout. Lusciou
desserts make a perfect finish. ❦ A good place (due to th
modest markup) to splurge on a fine wine from th
complete yet reasonable list.

AVERAGE DINNER FOR TWO: $6
Does not include wine, tax and gratuit

LE BEAUJOLAIS

131 PROVENCHER BLVD.
~ St. Boniface ~
WINNIPEG, MANITOBA
(204) 237-6276

Proprietor
VALERIE BODIROGA

Chef
COSTA

All major credit cards
Dinner Mon. to Sun. • Lunch Mon. to Fri.

MENU HIGHLIGHTS

★★★★★

APPETIZERS
PICKEREL CHEEKS WITH PERNOD
SAUCE • SCALLOPS WITH LEEKS
& SHALLOT SAUCE • FOUR-
LETTUCES SALAD WITH WARM
CAMEMBERT CHEESE &
RASPBERRY VINEGAR DRESSING

MAIN COURSES
DUCK WITH BLACK
CURRANT SAUCE (CASSIS)
& WILD RICE • RACK OF LAMB
NIÇOISE WITH RATATOUILLE
• BRAID OF SALMON & HALIBUT
WITH CILANTRO SAUCE

DESSERTS
ASSORTMENT OF
OUR CHEF'S PASTRIES

PORTAGE AND MAIN MAY BE ONE OF THE coldest places in the West, but just a half-mile across the bridge, owner Valerie Bodiroga's Le Beaujolais is unquestionably one of the warmest. ❦ By the refined lady's own admission, this lovely restaurant is her "baby". Genuine caring for guests and for everything that comes out of the kitchen is readily apparent. ❦ Garden flowers, quiet candlelight, views of the charmingly restored St. Boniface area, and, on Friday nights, an accomplished classical guitarist, all lend to the romantic calm of the 90-seat room. ❦ Remarkable attention to detail (the complimentary *choux* pastry starter filled with salmon mousse, for example) adds sparkle to this exceptional dining experience. ❦ The Chef, Costa, is master of an artful menu that ranges from Pickerel Cheeks Sautéed with Pernod and Leeks, or crackling-crisp Roast Duck, to superb, fresh Salmon in a Fresh Herb Vinaigrette. Breads are custom baked. Desserts are homemade and wickedly irresistible. ❦ Service is flawless, informed and attentive. ❦ Selected wines from the well-chosen list are available by the glass.

AVERAGE DINNER FOR TWO: $60
Does not include wine, tax and gratuity.

BETWEEN FRIENDS

1480 PEMBINA HIGHWAY
*Also located in Downtown Winnipeg,
in The Holiday Inn Crowne Plaza*
WINNIPEG, MANITOBA
(204) 284-8402

Executive Chef	Managing Partners
ELOI LOPES	JEAN-LOUIS DANGUY
	RAYMOND CHEVASSON

*All major credit cards
Dinner Mon. to Sun. • Lunch Mon. to Fri.*

MENU HIGHLIGHTS

★★★★★

APPETIZERS
CHICKEN LIVERS ON FRESH
SPINACH WITH RICOTTA CHEESE
• CARPACCIO OF SALMON WITH
DILL MUSTARD MARINADE

MAIN COURSES
3-CHEESE RAVIOLI WITH BASIL
& TOMATO SAUCE • FRESH
ATLANTIC SALMON IN VIRGIN
OLIVE OIL VINAIGRETTE •
VEAL SCALLOPINE TOPPED
WITH GULF SHRIMP &
LOBSTER BISQUE • ROAST
DUCK WITH MINAKI
BLUEBERRY

IN THE REALM OF FRENCH & ITALIAN COOKING nothing is impossible. At least not in the eyes of Managing Partners, Jean-Louis Danguy and Raymond Chevasson experienced restaurateurs whose aptly named Between Friends welcomes Winnipeg to informal weekday lunches and nightly dinners in a cheerful, multi-level room, winter-warmed by a huge fireplace. ❦ From hors d'oeuvres through desserts, Chef Eloi Lopes's extensive menu with a nightly table d'hôte selection teases the palate with choices both Italian and French: Carpaccio of Salmon with Dill Mustard Marinade; Veal Scallopine topped with Gulf Shrimp & Lobster Bisque. ❦ Off-the-menu personal favourites are prepared upon request "with enough notice", of course. ❦ An excellent wine list matches well with menu items. ❦ The dress code is casual, the atmosphere tasteful and congenial. Owner/patron tableside chats are almost a ritual. ❦ It is worth the 5-minute drive from downtown to search out this neighbourhood jewel. ❦ Valet parking, evenings.

AVERAGE DINNER FOR TWO: $55
Does not include wine, tax and gratuity

CONTINENTAL

Executive Chef
FRITZ ENGELHARD

Maître d'
PETER MALANDRAKIS

THE VELVET GLOVE

TWO LOMBARD PLACE
~ The Westin Hotel ~
WINNIPEG, MANITOBA
(204) 985-6255

All major credit cards
Dinner Mon. to Sun. • Lunch Mon. to Fri.

MENU HIGHLIGHTS

★★★★★

APPETIZERS
WINNIPEG GOLDEYE WITH LIME
VINAIGRETTE • SAUTÉED SEA
SCALLOPS ON PAPAYA BASIL
COULIS • PRAIRIE BLACK BEAN
SOUP

MAIN COURSES
PACIFIC SEAFOOD GRILL •
ROASTED VENISON WITH SUN-
DRIED CHERRY SAUCE & SWEET
POTATO PIE • SUPREME OF
CHICKEN AND ASPARAGUS IN
CHARDONNAY CREAM

DESSERTS
VELVET GLOVE RUM-FLAVOURED
CHOCOLATE TART • PAVLOVA
WITH FRESH STRAWBERRY COULIS

THE *CAA FOUR-DIAMOND* VELVET GLOVE IS AN elegant place for any occasion and a splendid value for this calibre of fine dining. ❦ Under the supremely capable direction of "everyone's favourite" Maitre d', Peter Malandrakis, the staff will ensure your every expectation is exceeded with style and panache. ❦ Harp music drifts through the lavishly panelled, fireside dining room while the creative kitchen of Executive Chef Fritz Engelhard contributes an elegance of its own. ❦ Dinners begin with an iced bucket of shrimp. Then a basket fresh with pumpernickel, sourdough, wheat breads. Famous starters here are the Prairie Black Bean Soup, and Smoked Winnipeg Goldeye with Lime Vinaigrette. Chef Engelhard's imaginative menus ensure wide appeal. ❦ The complete, expertly-chosen wine collection showcases wines from around the world. ❦ *Complimentary valet parking in the evening.*

AVERAGE DINNER FOR TWO: $55
Does not include wine, tax and gratuity.

ECLECTIC INTERNATIONAL

Proprietor
CLARK DAY

Chef
JACK FRANCIS

CLARK'S BY THE BAY

4085 BATH ROAD
~ 8 km west of Kingston on Hwy. 33 ~
KINGSTON (COLLINS BAY), ONTARIO
(613) 384-3551

All major credit cards
Dinner Monday to Saturday • Closed for lunch

MENU HIGHLIGHTS

★★★★★

APPETIZERS
THAI SEAFOOD BISQUE,
ESCARGOTS IN SPRING ROLL
PASTRY BASKET • PERSIAN
CHICKEN IN PHYLLO BUNDLE •
ITALIAN CHEESE SAMOSAS

MAIN COURSES
FRESH ATLANTIC SALMON
PAUPIETTES WITH LOBSTER
ARMORICAINE SAUCE • THAI
VEGETARIAN CURRY • RACK OF
LAMB ROSEMARY • BREAST OF
CHICKEN WITH LYCHEE, LEMON-
GRASS AND PINK PEPPERCORNS

DESSERTS
QUADRUPLE CHOCOLATE
CHEESECAKE • FRESH FRUIT
PHYLLO PASTRIES

INSIDE THIS HISTORIC 1832 VICTORIAN COUNTRY home set on, and overlooking, pretty Collins Bay near Kingston, the warmth of small rooms, open fireplaces, seasoned furniture and classical music set the scene for candlelight dining in the practiced style of resident hosts, Clark and Laurie Day. ❦ Champagne cocktails provide a fitting overture to Clark Day's fine and varied cuisine. Recommended is the multi-course table d'hôte, or, if you prefer, dine à la carte. Inventive specialties range from a Louisiana seafood dish and Paupiette of Salmon, all the way to a Vegetarian Thai Curry. Steak au Poivre brings preparation to your table. Desserts and pastries, the expert handiwork of Laurie Day, are purely decadent. ❦ The friendly, youthful service staff is fully capable of recommending wines (many available by the glass) complementary to each course. ❦ Ontario's finer wines are prominent on the well-chosen wine list, alongside a rewarding (and realistically priced) international collection. ❦ For a fine dining break on the tedious drive between Montreal and Toronto, mark this oasis on your map.

AVERAGE DINNER FOR TWO: $55
Does not include wine, tax and gratuity.

Proprietor
TONY PEREIRA

Sous-Chef
BEVAN TERRY
Head Chef
OLAF MERTENS

ROGUES

1900 DUNDAS ST. WEST
~ Sherwood Forest Shopping Village,
between Erin Mills Parkway and Mississauga Road ~
MISSISSAUGA, ONTARIO
(905) 822-2670

All major credit cards
Dinner Monday to Saturday • Lunch Monday to Friday

MENU HIGHLIGHTS

★★★★★

APPETIZERS
SHRIMPS FLAMBÉED IN BRANDY
• EGGPLANT WITH BOCCONCCINI
CHEESE BAKED WITH TOMATO
BASIL SAUCE • CAPRESE SALAD

MAIN COURSES
PAGLIA E FIENO (SAUTÉED SMOKED
SALMON, FLAMBÉED IN VODKA AND
GREEN PEPPERCORNS, SERVED WITH
A TOMATO CREAM SAUCE) •
AGNOLOTTI PASTA STUFFED WITH
RICOTTA, SPINACH AND CHIVES,
SERVED WITH A ROSÉ SAUCE •
GRILLED VEAL TENDERLOIN
MEDALLIONS AND GRILLED SHRIMP
IN A RED WINE SAUCE • ROASTED
RACK OF LAMB MARINATED IN
MUSTARD, HERBS AND SPICES

TUCKED AWAY IN EXCLUSIVE SHERWOOD Forest Village, a shopping plaza as haute as they come outside of Toronto, Rogues sets the standard for warm, energetic, suburban dining. ❦ In a villa environment of rosy brick and imported European tiles, spirited conversation and laughter is underlined by the pungent scent of garlic emanating from the open kitchen that is the restaurant's centrepiece. Proprietor Tony Pereira (formerly of the Windsor Arms and Millcroft Inn) will almost certainly be on hand to greet you personally and escort you through the garden of greenery that separates the large restaurant into cozy niches dressed in rose and white linen. ❦ German-trained Chef, Olaf Mertens (soon to achieve his Culinary Master degree in Europe), choreographs the work of eight staff chefs and loves the open kitchen's proximity to guests every bit as much as guests do. Menus are all à la carte, and, to please a vast following of regulars, offer an extensive selection of beautifully prepared specialties. ❦ Italian, French and Californian wines dominate the excellent wine list. The son of a Portugese winemaker, Tony is quite a collector as evidenced by his specialty list which includes 19th century cognacs and ports.

AVERAGE DINNER FOR TWO: $60
Does not include wine, tax and gratuity.

ON THE TWENTY

3836 MAIN STREET
~ QEW west towards Niagara, Vineland exit ~
JORDAN, ONTARIO
(905) 562-7313

Chef
MICHAEL OLSON

Manager
DON DYSON
Proprietor
HELEN YOUNG

Visa and Mastercard
Dinner and Lunch Tuesday to Sunday

MENU HIGHLIGHTS

APPETIZERS
CHARDONNAY-SMOKED
SHORTHILLS TROUT WITH
BEETROOT-HORSERADISH RELISH •
GRILLED VEAL AND FENNEL
SAUSAGE ON SMOKY EGGPLANT
SALAD

MAIN COURSES
CINNAMON-SCENTED SMITHVILLE
DUCK BREAST ON GINGER-BLACK
CURRANT SAUCE • LAMB SHANK
BRAISED IN GAMAY NOIR WITH
ROSEMARY-SCENTED WHITE BEANS •
YELLOWFIN TUNA WITH BLACK
OLIVE VINAIGRETTE AND RED
PEPPER CATSUP

DESSERT
RED HAVEN PEACH CAKE WITH
CULP ROAD BERRY SAUCE

ON THE TWENTY IS ONTARIO'S FIRST WINERY restaurant, a one-of-a-kind find in a relaxed country setting, named for its picturesque proximity to Twenty Mile Creek. ✸ It shares space in an historic 19th-century winery with Ontario's leading V.Q.A. vintner, Cave Spring Cellars. ✸ As outspoken as the distinguished wine maker in its commitment to the unique flavours of the luscious Niagara harvest, On The Twenty has pioneered the shaping of this fertile region's own cuisine. ✸ From the fold of Toronto's elite chefs, Chef Michael Olson admits to being overwhelmed by the bounty of local fruits, vegetables, meats and fish available here. Dealing directly with growers as close to Jordan as possible, he knows the origin and quality of his ingredients, and he knows how to unite them with traditional and modern techniques vibrant with imagination. ✸ A *prix fixé* "Winemaker's Luncheon" marries finely appropriate Cave Spring Cellars V.Q.A. wine with exciting courses that include the likes of Forest Mushrooms Baked in Parchment and Salad of Bob Patterson Greens in Vineland Sour Cherry Dressing. Conclude perhaps with Whistle Hill Matsu Apple & Almond Strudel with Caramel Ice Cream & Vanilla Custard Sauce. Or, if you prefer, select from the à la carte menu

AVERAGE DINNER FOR TWO: $70
Does not include wine, tax and gratuity

CLASSICAL FRENCH

CHEZ JEAN PIERRE

210 SOMERSET STREET WEST
~ Ottawa centre ~
OTTAWA, ONTARIO
(613) 235-9711

Chef & Proprietor JEAN PIERRE MULLER	Co-proprietor RACHEL MULLER	*All major credit cards* *Dinner Tuesday to Saturday • Lunch Tuesday to Friday*

MENU HIGHLIGHTS

★★★★★

APPETIZERS
LOBSTER BISQUE •
SWEETBREADS IN PUFF PASTRY
WITH WHITE WINE SAUCE
• SCALLOPS AND SNAILS IN
ROQUEFORT SAUCE WITH
WALNUTS

MAIN COURSES
DOVER SOLE MEUNIÈRE •
SHRIMPS SAUTÉED WITH GARLIC
AND COGNAC • TOURNEDOS
WITH WILD MUSHROOMS • VEAL
TENDERLOIN WITH SLICED
LOBSTER • BONED QUAIL
STUFFED WITH FOIE GRAS,
SERVED IN A POTATO NEST
WITH GARNISHING

"QUINTESSENTIALLY FRENCH — AND FABUlous" says *EnRoute Magazine* of Jean Pierre and Rachel Muller's outstanding Chez Jean Pierre restaurant. We agree. ❦ Jean Pierre (whose background includes tenure as Cuisinier at the Governor General's residence and 17 years at the U.S. Embassy residence) is a master in the kitchen. Trends, fads and contemporary short-cuts to classical French cuisine have no place here. Refusing to compromise traditional ways, Jean Pierre consistently turns the freshest of ingredients into practiced elegance. ❦ Like a rose on the ground floor of an anonymous, city-central highrise, the splendidly appointed dining room, personally overseen by Rachel Muller, is a compliment to its guests. Expect such creature comforts as fine linen, silver, fresh flowers, candlelight, and a formally-outfitted service staff. When time permits, Jean Pierre will leave the kitchen to share a moment with guests. ❦ In the best French tradition, management/staff teamwork is so fine-tuned that the restaurant "family" dines together early each evening to discuss menus and restaurant matters. ❦ Equally fine-tuned is the exclusively French wine list.

AVERAGE DINNER FOR TWO: $60
Does not include wine, tax and gratuity.

FRENCH BISTRO

CLAIR DE LUNE

81B CLARENCE STREET
~ Adjacent to Ottawa's famous Byward Market ~
OTTAWA, ONTARIO
(613) 230-2200

Proprietor
ADEL AYAD

Chef
IAN THOMPSON

All major credit cards
Dinner Monday to Sunday
Lunch Monday to Friday (Brunch Saturday & Sunday)

MENU HIGHLIGHTS

★★★★★

APPETIZERS
FRESH AND SMOKED SALMON
RILLETTES • SAUTÉED SHRIMPS
WITH LENTILS AND CHICK PEAS,
SWEET GARLIC, ONIONS,
BALSAMIC VINEGAR AND CHILI
OIL • RISOTTO WITH THREE
MUSHROOMS AND PARMESAN

MAIN COURSES
CRISP ROAST CHICKEN BREAST
WITH CURRY AND THREE
CHUTNEYS • BARBECUE PORK
TENDERLOIN WITH APRICOT
GLAZE, YAM AND PANCETTA
PURÉE • BEEF TENDERLOIN
MEDALLIONS WITH PEPPER, WILD
MUSHROOMS AND BEAUJOLAIS
JUS, SERVED WITH RISOTTO

AFTER BYWARD MARKET'S SEDUCTIVE, garden-fresh bounty and festive energy ignite your appetite, head for the Clair de Lune Restaurant/Bistro on nearby Clarence Street. ❦ Ever-present owner (and former Research Scientist), Adel Ayad, is the driving force here. Adel selects the table d'hôte and à la carte menus; sometimes lends a hand in the kitchen; knows virtually everybody in Ottawa; and always "goes the extra mile" for his guests. ❦ There's a pleasant sense of "neighbourhood" here. To your left and right as you enter from street level, the casual, chic and very friendly "bistro" is warmed with a happy mix of locals and visitors. Elevated and separate from the bistro are two small, equally welcoming dining areas. ❦ Young, capable, and Western Canadian, Chef Ian Thompson demonstrates flexibility, quality and character in his market-fresh presentations (check out the "catch-of-the-day"). Lunch is a bargain. At dinner the kitchen shines. ❦ The bright, engaging service staff knows its business, remembers customers by name, and contributes much to the congeniality. ❦ A superb selection by the glass headlines the complete wine list. ❦ Live jazz Saturday nights. Light summer dinners served on the popular rooftop terrace.

AVERAGE DINNER FOR TWO: $55
Does not include wine, tax and gratuity.

NORTHERN ITALIAN

Proprietors & Chefs
Ron Falsetti
Geraldo Gnassi

Maître d'
Fidel Guzman

GERALDO'S RISTORANTE ITALIANO

200 BEECHWOOD AVENUE
~ Vanier, 5-minute drive from city centre ~
OTTAWA, ONTARIO
(613) 747-0272

All major credit cards
Dinner Tuesday to Sunday • Lunch Tuesday to Friday

MENU HIGHLIGHTS

★★★★★

APPETIZERS
CARPACCIO DI MANZO •
CALAMARI FRITTI • LUMACHI
CON FUNGHI

MAIN COURSES
RAVIOLI ALLA FIORENTINA
• VITELLO ALLA PAIARDA
• FRESH "CATCH OF THE DAY"
• BISTECCA ALLA PIZZAIOLA

DESSERT
TIRAMISOU

AN OTTAWA DINING EXPERIENCE NOT TO BE missed is Geraldo's, not for the decor, not for the locale, but for mouth-watering antipasti; perfect hand-made pastas; veal dishes both delicate and lightly volcanic; and exquisite, velvety sauces. Half-orders are a thoughtful option not often offered elsewhere. Bread is delivered warm to the table by one of a friendly, helpful service team. ❦ Well-liked by both customers and peers, Owner/Chef Geraldo (Gerry) Gnassi is the youthful, personable force behind this restaurant's success. Freshness is paramount in his kitchen. Daily trips to the market are often punctuated with visits to his own herb garden. ❦ In this location for three years, Geraldo's began when Gerry Gnassi, with the help of his family and friends, turned a rundown duplex into a restaurant for a total of 82 diners, upstairs and down. With the modest, casual character of a family-owned, neighbourhood dining room, and arguably the finest Italian food in eastern Ontario, Geraldo's has attracted the attention of the *New York Times*, and locally has earned its place as the darling of reviewers. ❦ Italian wines, by the glass, half-litre or bottle.

AVERAGE DINNER FOR TWO: $55
Does not include wine, tax and gratuity.

Proprietor
PHILIP LAI

Manager
GRACE LAI

Hostess
ALICE LAI

SIAM BISTRO

1268 WELLINGTON STREET
~ Near Holland Avenue ~
OTTAWA, ONTARIO
(613) 728-3111

All major credit cards
Dinner Monday to Sunday
Lunch Monday to Friday

THE FOOD IS THE STAR IN THIS OUT-OF-THE-way little treasure just five minutes from the Parliament Buildings. The superbly-balanced offerings of sweet and sour, lemon grass, ginger, chilies, garlic and basil are, quite simply, outstanding. Prices are reasonable; portions honest. "The best meal I've ever had in Ottawa..." said one local reviewer. ❦ Very informal, Siam Bistro, owned by Philip and Alice Lai, offers 50 diners a refined, tranquil dining environment awash with gentle oriental music and soft candlelight. White stucco walls background an ever-changing art display centred around a striking Burmese wallhanging, intricate with sparkling stones and beading. ❦ Alice Lai is your hostess. The hospitality is genuine, backed up with quiet, gracious, traditionally-costumed service. Families, couples and single diners all frequent Siam Bistro. ❦ Although the wine list is unusually complete for a Thai restaurant, some maintain that the best wine with Thai food is beer. Siam Bistro features beer imports from 15 countries (including Tsingtao from China). ❦ *Philip and Alice also own Ottawa's Siam Kitchen (Thai) and Ta Tung Dining Lounge (Szechuan) restaurants.*

46

AVERAGE DINNER FOR TWO: $40
Does not include wine, tax and gratuity.

MODERN FRENCH

RUNDLES

9 COBOURG STREET
~ Downtown ~
STRATFORD, ONTARIO
(519) 271-6442

Proprietor
JAMES MORRIS

Chef
NEIL BAXTER

All major credit cards
Dinner Tuesday to Sunday
Lunch Wednesday, Saturday & Sunday

MENU HIGHLIGHTS

★★★★★

APPETIZERS
BAKED STUFFED ARTICHOKES WITH
PROVENÇAL GARLIC MAYONNAISE
• WARM SCALLOP AND CELERY
ROOT SALAD

MAIN COURSES
ATLANTIC SALMON WITH A POTATO
CRUST, CARAMELIZED ONIONS
AND LOBSTER SAUCE • CRISP,
SUCCULENT CONFIT OF DUCK •
ROAST SADDLE OF VENISON WITH
WILD MUSHROOM AND POTATO
CAKE, AND ROAST VEGETABLES

DESSERTS
CARAMELIZED VANILLA CREAM •
BITTERSWEET CHOCOLATE TART
WITH ORANGE SORBET

MANY WHO KNOW THIS ENCHANTING TOWN consider Rundles as important an element of their visits here as the famous Stratford Shakespearean Festival, and rightly so, for Rundles can stand alone as a Stratford attraction. ❧ Rundles reflects the genuine passion for food and the arts of its soft-spoken owner, James Morris. The restaurant resides in a superbly decorated, summer-cool house set by the pretty Avon River adrift with swans. The environment is perfect for lingering over market-inspired three-course meals from the expert kitchen of well-known Chef, Neil Baxter. ❧ Creative variety is the keynote here, with splendid combinations of tastes light-handedly prepared, and arranged with a remarkable sensitivity to detail. Ever-evolving through experimentation, Baxter's "disarming creations" have earned the attention of *Gourmet* and other important magazines, with special tributes paid to the grilled vegetable terrine and crispy-skin confit of duck; beautiful grilled and cold poached salmon; perfectly seared shellfish coins; and "showstopper vegetables." ❧ Carefully chosen wines comprise an international selection.

47

AVERAGE DINNER FOR TWO: $100
Does not include wine, tax and gratuity.

FRENCH "MODERNE"

General Manager
SCOTT WILLOWS

Sous-Chefs
LILI SULLIVAN
JOHN CURTIS

AUBERGE DU POMMIER

4150 YONGE STREET
~ South of Highway 401 ~
TORONTO (YORK MILLS), ONTARIO
(416) 222-2220

All major credit cards
Dinner Monday to Saturday • Lunch Monday to Friday

MENU HIGHLIGHTS

★★★★★

APPETIZERS
PAN-SEARED PROVIMI
SWEETBREADS ON A CRISP
MILLEFEUILLE • SAGE-ROASTED
SEA SCALLOPS WITH PANCETTA ON
CREAMY CHARRED CORN RISOTTO •
DUCK BREAST ON MUSTARD SLAW
AND CITRUS VINAIGRETTE

MAIN COURSES
ROASTED RACK OF VENISON WITH A
SMOKY EGGPLANT TART • GRILLED
FILLET OF MAHI MAHI • ROASTED
LAMB LOIN WITH A SUN-DRIED
TOMATO AND OLIVE CRUST •
BREAST OF GUINEA FOWL WITH A
SHRIMP AND MOREL MOUSSELINE •
SOY-ROASTED SALMON FILLET •
GRILLED AGED BEEF TENDERLOIN

TORONTO'S NOTED ENTREPRENEURIAL RES
taurateur, Peter Oliver, created the atmosphere of a qui
French country inn when he merged two forme
groundskeeper cottages to create this 160-seat jewel of
restaurant. His stated goal was to make Auberge d
Pommier the city's finest — and the loyal clientele wh
make the Auberge their "oasis" appreciate his efforts. ❦
Three distinctly different dining rooms offer the romanti
ambiance of cozy fireplaces and oak-beamed, yet contem
porary decor. The Terrace seats 60 in an equally inspirin
two-level garden setting. ❦ The cuisine is Frenc
"moderne" with changing menu choices of fowl, veniso
fresh-caught fish and seasonal shellfish, in addition t
savory beef and lamb dishes. ❦ The expert service, led b
General Manager Scott Willows, is friendly and attentiv
the overall excellence is reflected in the high acclai
earned from both *EnRoute Magazine* and British Airway
❦ The wine list has depth in French choices, and bread
in Italian and West Coast American. Fine private impo
tations, Premier Cru, and Bordeaux vintages from gre
years can be found, and fully enjoyed.

AVERAGE DINNER FOR TWO: $8
Does not include wine, tax and gratuit

BANGKOK GARDEN

18 ELM STREET
~ Downtown, northwest of Dundas and Yonge ~
TORONTO, ONTARIO
(416) 977-6748

Proprietor	Manager	All major credit cards
SHERRY BRYDSON	AVI KULKARNI	Dinner Monday to Sunday • Lunch Monday to Friday
	Chef	
	PAYOONG KLINPROONG	

MENU HIGHLIGHTS

★★★★★

APPETIZERS
TOM YUM GOONG (LEMON SHRIMP
SOUP) • PRIK YOUAK YOD SAI
(STEAMED BANANA PEPPERS FILLED
WITH PORK, THAI CHILLIES AND
HOT SAUCE) • YUM NUA (BEEF
TENDERLOIN SLICES TOSSED WITH
ROASTED RICE, SHALLOTS, CHILLIES,
MINT AND DRESSED IN LIME JUICE)

ASSORTED DISHES
GANG MUSSAMAN (TAMARIND
CURRY) • PLA LAAD PRIK (DEEP-
FRIED FISH IN A FIERY CHILLI
CORIANDER SAUCE) • PAD THAI
(THAI RICE NOODLES) • KANOM
JEAN NAM PRIK (SOFT NOODLES,
CRISP VEGETABLES AND PIQUANT
COCONUT CURRY SAUCE)

AFTER YEARS OF LIVING IN THAILAND AND loving its culture and cuisine, Sherry Brydson returned and opened Toronto's premier Thai restaurant with authenticity and elegance. Twelve years and numerous awards later, Bangkok Garden (blessed at its opening by Thai Buddhist monks) is still a showpiece. ❧ The two-storey garden atmosphere is exotic: polished teakwood, lush tropical greenery, and a river. Waiters are costumed, helpful and always unobtrusive. ❧ The chefs are direct from Thailand. So, too, is the tableware. ❧ Dinners are an adventure. Great attention is paid to detail (guests often ask to take home the exquisite vegetable sculpture garnishes). Bangkok Garden's cuisine is healthful, exciting and inspired by centuries of Thai culinary tradition. In fact, ingredients that are unavailable here are flown in from Bangkok. Freshness shines through meticulously assembled offerings. The satays are memorable. The spicy dishes, genuine. ❧ Good wine list. ❧ *Also reommended is The Noodle Bar at The Brass Flamingo, situated directly below Bangkok Garden at street level.*

AVERAGE DINNER FOR TWO: $65
Does not include wine, tax and gratuity.

NORTHERN INDIAN

BOMBAY PALACE

71 JARVIS STREET
~ Downtown ~
TORONTO, ONTARIO
(416) 368-8048

Proprietor
IQBAL CHATWAL

Manager
I.P. SINGH

All major credit cards
Dinner and Lunch Monday to Sunday

MENU HIGHLIGHTS

★★★★★

APPETIZERS
ONION BHAJIA
• ASSORTED PLATTER

MAIN COURSES
BUTTER CHICKEN • LAMB
CHOPS KHANDAHARI
• SEAFOOD VINDALLO
• SALI BOTI • PALACE
SIZZLING GRILL

DESSERTS
RAS MALAI •
GULAB JAMAN
• MANGO ICE CREAM

OVER 20 YEARS AGO, IQBAL CHATWAL opened his first Bombay Palace in downtown Montreal. It has been a trusted favourite ever since, expanding its proven recipe for success to locations in New York, Los Angeles, Budapest and Hong Kong as well as Toronto. ❦ In every location, Bombay Palace has earned a vast and loyal following, from the younger generation who appreciate affordable, healthful fare, to the older and more worldly who recognize the restaurant's quality, enjoy its dining excellence and appreciate its refined and friendly ambiance. Toronto's Bombay Palace, serving 150 under the guidance of Manager I.P. Singh, is no exception. ❦ In addition to a mouthwatering selection of tandoori entrées ovenbaked Punjabi style, Bombay Palace caters to the growing heart- and health-conscious crowd with a special menu of exceptional low-cholesterol dishes that retain every nuance of smoky, spicy flavour. ❦ Every item on the tempting menu is a trustworthy dining adventure; every sauce a unique and flavourful delight. ❦ *Bombay Palace's other Toronto-area locations: 35 Dundas St. W., Mississauga (Tel. 566-4940) and 795 Markham Rd., Scarborough (Tel. 431-5577).*

AVERAGE DINNER FOR TWO: $35
Does not include wine, tax and gratuity.

EASTERN MEDITERRANEAN

Proprietor
MICHAEL CARLEVALE

General Manager
BRENT DE KLERCK

BYZANTIUM

499 CHURCH STREET
~ Downtown, just east of Yonge Street ~
TORONTO, ONTARIO
(416) 922-3859

All major credit cards
Dinner Monday to Sunday • Closed for lunch
(Brunch Sunday)

MENU HIGHLIGHTS

★★★★★

APPETIZERS
DAILY PLATE OF DIPS • EGGPLANT
ANTIPASTO • DEEP-FRIED
ARTICHOKES • PERSIAN SPICED
CHICKEN IN PASTRY • DEEP-FRIED
CALAMARI

MAIN COURSES
NEW YORK SIRLOIN • VEAL IN THE
MOOD OF THE CHEF • CHICKEN
TAGINE • FISH OF THE DAY •
COUSCOUS WITH VEGETABLES •
BARLEY RISOTTO • SICILIAN
SEAFOOD PASTA

DESSERTS
BAKLAVA AND OTHER PASTRY,
MADE IN-HOUSE

IN THE LIVELY AND COLOURFUL AREA JUST east of Yonge Street that's recognized as "the gay area of downtown," everyone is welcomed into Byzantium's two slender rooms. The lively bar seats 22. The dining room can accommodate 75 with care and flair, at tables comfortably lit by stained-glass lamps. Glowing with burnished copper, silvers and golds, the mosaic decor and bold table settings reflect the wit and artistry of Owner Michael Carlevale. ❦ Superbly presented Eastern Mediterranean cuisine has placed Byzantium at the forefront of fashionable dining, and earned an admirable 3 1/2-star rating from *Toronto Life* magazine. ❦ General Manager, Brent de Klerck, a decade-long sidekick of Carlevale, oversees a competent and congenial service team. ❦ The thoughtful menu with its emphasis on white meats and fishes, vegetables and grains, is organized by Mediterranean region: Greek, Italian and Levantine choices arrive on generous platters (perfect for sampling and sharing) alongside selections from Turkey, Lebanon or North Africa. ❦ Complementing the menu, the 60-label wine list is divided between light and spicy wines and light flavourful reds.

AVERAGE DINNER FOR TWO: $60
Does not include wine, tax and gratuity.

Proprietor
FRANCO PREVEDELLO

Chef
MARC THUET

CENTRO GRILL & WINE BAR

2472 YONGE ST.
~ Midtown, north of Eglington Ave. ~
TORONTO, ONTARIO
(416) 483-2211

All major credit cards
Dinner Monday to Saturday • Closed for lunch

MENU HIGHLIGHTS

★★★★★

APPETIZERS
TERRINE OF FOIE GRAS WITH
GREEN BEAN SALAD AND MANGO
VINAIGRETTE • SWORDFISH
CARPACCIO WITH ORIENTAL
EGGPLANT CAVIAR • SPINACH-
RICOTTA GNOCCHI IN A RAGOUT
OF SWEETBREADS

MAIN COURSES
RACK OF LAMB WITH
GREMOLADA JUS AND MINT AIOLI
• GRILLED PROVIMI VEAL CHOP
IN A CHIVE-MUSHROOM SAUCE
WITH OLIVE MASHED POTATOES
• ZUPPA DI PESCE (FISH AND
SEAFOOD IN A WINE-CORIANDER
BROTH, SERVED FRIDAYS ONLY)

EXPECT GREAT THINGS FROM RESTAURANT dynamo Franco Prevedello who, after his success with Pronto, brought the city Centro, Splendido and Acrobat. ❦ Centro, one of Toronto's most enduringly popular dining spots among the chic and celebrated, is big, bold, and hums with energy beneath the music of the resident piano. Bright with skylights, high ceilings, mirrors, powerful colours and visuals, Centro happily accommodates 200 casually well-dressed patrons on two levels, more in the Wine Bar. ❦ Formerly of the Windsor Arms and here for five years, Chef Marc Thuet's menus (which change regularly) are dazzling. Flavours are robust and confident. Inventive combinations (Caramelized Breast of Free Range Chicken in Port Jus, or Spiced Swordfish Tournedos with Niçoise Olive Ratatouille & Lime-Ginger Butter for example) work like a dream. Presentation is pure art. Pasta dishes are exciting and for the pizza afficionado, there's a nightly choice from the wood-burning oven. Be sure to sample Pastry Chef David Castellan's brilliant desserts. ❦ Service is smiling, smart and highly praised. ❦ The international wine selection (many by the glass) is complete and seductive with an assortment of lovely barolos.

AVERAGE DINNER FOR TWO: $80
Does not include wine, tax and gratuity.

CHIADO

864 COLLEGE STREET
~ Downtown, Little Portugal district ~
TORONTO, ONTARIO
(416) 538-1910

Co-proprietor ALBINO SILVA	Chef MANUEL VILELA	*All major credit cards* *Dinner and Lunch Monday to Sunday*

MENU HIGHLIGHTS

★★★★★

APPETIZERS
GRILLED SQUID WITH ROASTED
PEPPERS • MARINATED SARDINES
WITH LEMON AND PARSLEY
SERVED RAW OR GRILLED •
STEAMED CLAMS BULHAO PATO
• ROASTED BREAST OF CAPON
OVER FRESH GREENS

MAIN COURSES
VARIETY OF FISH (FLOWN IN
FRESH FROM PORTUGAL) ON THE
GRILL • GRILLED TIGER SHRIMP
COM PIRIPIRI • ACORDA DE
MARISCO

DESSERTS
VARIETY OF HOMEMADE
TRADITIONAL SWEETS

NAMED FOR THE OLDEST NEIGHBOURHOOD in Lisbon and just over two years old itself, charming little Chiado is the newest star in Toronto's gastronomic galaxy. ❦ Pet project of consummate restaurateur, Albino Silva (who taught at the American Culinary Institute) and Gino Ferreira, Chiado merges ochre walls and dark wood into a bright, warm, bistro setting in the colourful Portuguese area of town. ❦ A frontrunner in the evolution of Portuguese cuisine (both cosmopolitan and regional), Chiado features uniquely prepared meals from Chef Silva's innovative, diverse kitchen. His modern approach and traditional methods produce a fine assortment of starters, and main courses that range from grilled squid, roasted breast of free-range capon, and Portuguese bistretto-style steak; to rack of lamb, rabbit, grilled tiger shrimp and excellent fresh fish (much of which is flown in from Portugal). ❦ Breads, pastries and desserts are all prepared in Chiado's kitchen and bakery. ❦ An extensive selection of Portuguese wines (especially reds), and ports by the three-ounce glass highlight a complete wine list.

AVERAGE DINNER FOR TWO: $55
Does not include wine, tax and gratuity.

MODERN INTERNATIONAL

LE CONTINENTAL

900 YORK MILLS ROAD
~ 10 minutes from Downtown Toronto,
in The Toronto Prince Hotel ~
TORONTO (NORTH YORK), ONTARIO
(416) 444-2511

| Executive Chef | Restaurant Manager | *All major credit cards* |
| HANS ULRICH HERZIG | JEAN-PIERRE CENTENO | *Dinner Monday to Saturday • Lunch Monday to Friday* |

MENU HIGHLIGHTS

★★★★★

APPETIZERS
MILLEFEUILLE OF SALMON WITH
RIESLING AND CHIVE

MAIN COURSES
ARCTIC CHAR EN PAPILLOTE •
ROASTED VEAL CHOP WITH
ROSEMARY AND MUSHROOM
RISOTTO • ROASTED BREAST OF
DUCK ON AGED PORT WINE •
FILET MIGNON OF BEEF, GRILLED
OR PAN-FRIED, WITH SHALLOT
COMPOTE

DESSERTS
RICH ASSORTMENT OF DOMESTIC
AND IMPORTED CHEESES •
SABAYON WITH MARSALA AND
SEASONAL BERRIES

LE CONTINENTAL EMERGED GLORIOUSLY from its renovation cocoon on September 15, 1993, not only with an innovative new look but with the culinary mastery of gold medal Chef, Hans Ulrich Herzig; the formidable management talents of Jean-Pierre Centeno (Fenton's, Pronto, Centro, La Fenice); and the extraordinary expertise of wine specialist, John Defreitas. The combination is dynamite. ❦ Informal, friendly, un-stuffy is the attitude in this gentle ultra-tech environment. The centerpiece of the main dining room is a remarkable climate-controlled wine pavilion within which guests are invited to browse the impressive collection. Trust the advice of wine authorities Jean-Pierre or John; far from selling pricey wine, their interest lies in affordably delighting the palate, by the glass or by the bottle. ❦ The ambitious à la carte menu created by Chef Herzig (formerly of Toronto's famous Windsor Arms), sparkles with originality and a wisdom for balance. Freshness is paramount. Presentation is artful. Enthusiastic service is discreetly lighthearted, yet correct. ❦ The marble-ceilinged, African darkwood-panelled room lined with windows, overlooks acres of forest by day; city lights by night, when live piano stylings lend to the experience.

AVERAGE DINNER FOR TWO: $80
Does not include wine, tax and gratuity.

LA FENICE

319 KING ST. WEST
~ Downtown, Theatre District ~
TORONTO, ONTARIO
(416) 585-2377

Proprietor & Executive Chef
LUIGI ORGERA

Chef
ROBERTO FLORINDI

All major credit cards
Dinner Monday to Saturday • Lunch Monday to Friday

MENU HIGHLIGHTS

★★★★★

APPETIZERS
TROLLEY FILLED WITH A
VARIETY OF DELICACIES

MAIN COURSES
SELECTION OF FRESH-GRILLED,
SALT-WATER FISH • PASTA AL
DENTE • VEAL DISHES •
SEASONAL SPECIALTIES
(BISON, BOAR, FOWL) •
A FABULOUS VARIETY OF
MUSHROOMS, INCLUDING
TRUFFLES, WHITE AND BLACK,
DRESSED WITH EXTRA-VIRGIN
OLIVE OIL FROM LA FENICE'S
OWN ITALIAN OLIVE GROVE

IN THIS CITY REPUTED TO HAVE THE LARGEST Italian population outside of Italy, posh little La Fenice (pronounced La Fen-EE-chay) has been credited locally as "the most authentic Italian restaurant in Toronto" and Owner/Chef Luigi Orgera, for 30 years a star in the Toronto restaurant firmament, spares no effort to keep it that way. ❦ Terracotta tiles, marble tables, stylish artwork and classical music nurture the setting, but it is the superb fresh produce, exquisite home-made pasta, milk-fed veal, and especially the market-fresh fish and shellfish that continue to attract theatre-goers, power lunchers, and serious diners. ❦ Everything is fresh. Fish, selected by you at your table, is prepared simply, with extra-virgin olive oil imported from Orgera's own Italian olive grove, and herbs from his private garden. Antipasto (also served at the downstairs pasta and dessert bar) is a highlight that includes marinated fresh salmon, roasted peppers, zucchini and eggplant, calamari, shrimp, marinated octopus. Lavish desserts, also made on the premises, are often brilliant. Service, led by Maître d', Adriano Vincentini, is excellent, of course. ❦ An incredible wine list emphasizes Italian wines (many by the glass), beers, mineral waters, and a breathtaking selection of grappas.

AVERAGE DINNER FOR TWO: $80
Does not include wine, tax and gratuity.

JUMP CAFÉ & BAR

1 WELLINGTON STREET WEST
~ Downtown, Commerce Court East - Court Level
(entrance off Wellington, west of Yonge St.) ~
TORONTO, ONTARIO
(416) 363-3400 • FAX: (416) 363-3830

Co-Proprietor   Executive Chef
MICHAEL BONACINI MARTIN KOUPRIE

All major credit cards
Dinner Monday to Saturday • Lunch Monday to Friday

MENU HIGHLIGHTS

★★★★★

APPETIZERS
BAKED GOAT CHEESE SALAD •
GRILLED CALAMARI • PINE ISLAND
OYSTERS ON THE HALF SHELL WITH
TEQUILA GRAPEFRUIT • ANGEL HAIR
PASTA WITH GRILLED DEEP SEA
SCALLOPS • PIZZA BIANCA WITH
PESTO, SMOKED MOZZARELLA,
PROSCIUTTO, POTATOES AND
ROASTED PEPPERS

MAIN COURSES
STRIPLOIN OF BLACK ANGUS •
RISOTTO WITH GRILLED BLACK
TIGER SHRIMPS • GRILLED AND
BURNED GROUPER IN TURMERIC AND
GINGER • ROAST RACK OF LAMB
WITH CLOVE MUSTARD HERB CRUST,
WHITE TURNIP PURÉE AND RICE
WINE VINEGAR JUS

THE MOMENT ACCLAIMED TORONTO RESTAU-
rateur, Peter Oliver, and new partner, Superchef Michael
Bonacini, declared Jump "open," it became an instant hit
with the downtown office and theatre crowds. This hip
café/bar is definitely worth finding amid the maze of
Commerce Court, where the airy atrium setting embraces
expertly crafted dining by Executive Chef, Martin Kouprie.
❦ "Exciting" is no understatement for a dining experience
enhanced by the café's high energy level plus the friendly
competence of the serving staff ready with insightful
suggestions to food and wine. Parties of 40 to 200 can be
accommodated, and arrangements made for semi-private
dining. ❦ The atmosphere is electric; the cuisine eclectic.
Here you'll find an astonishing blend of choices and the
best of both worlds East and West — even a special Tapas
menu for patrons of the lively, and usually crowded, bar
area. ❦ Beyond its visual impact and exquisite culinary
temptations, Jump knows wine. Adding to an extensive
wine list covering the world's most important regions
(including Ontario) are over a dozen excellent selections
available by the glass.

AVERAGE DINNER FOR TWO: $70
Does not include wine, tax and gratuity.

JAPANESE

KATSURA

900 YORK MILLS ROAD
~ West of Don Mills Road,
in the Toronto Prince Hotel ~
TORONTO (NORTH YORK), ONTARIO
(416) 444-2511

Chef
HIROO MITSUI

Managers
DAVID LO
REIKO MURAMATSU

All major credit cards
Dinner Monday to Sunday • Lunch Monday to Friday

MENU HIGHLIGHTS

★★★★★

APPETIZERS
ASSORTED TEMPURA • ASSORTED
SUSHI • CHICKEN YAKITORI

MAIN COURSES
KATSURA SPECIAL MORIAWASE
(TEMPURA SHRIMPS AND
VEGETABLES, CHICKEN BROCHETTES
AND BROILED SIRLOIN TERIYAKI
WITH ASSORTED VEGETABLES) •
STEAK AND LOBSTER COMBINATION
(BROILED FILET MIGNON AND ROCK
LOBSTER TAIL SERVED WITH
VEGETABLES)

DESSERTS
GREEN TEA ICE CREAM • PARFAIT
MOUNT FUJI CUP (GREEN TEA
SYRUP ON ICE CREAM WITH
MITSUMAME)

THROUGH THE GATES OF KATSURA, YOU'RE welcomed as an honoured guest into a gentle garden atmosphere where Japanese cookery is presented in a multitude of classic ways. ❦ Look on the second level for the sushi bar with 14 seats and four tables for four. ❦ Elsewhere, there's a robata yaki (grilled fish) counter, a tempura bar, private tatami rooms, and conventional seating. Discreet dividers and varying levels personalize the room's size; dramatic lighting, candlelight and fresh flowers lend romance. The flashing, dancing knives of expert chefs provide an entertainment in themselves. ❦ Complete multi-course dinners are offered, alongside a complex and far-reaching à la carte menu with no fewer than a dozen categories from which to choose. Fish and seafood specialties include sole; fried scallops and shrimp teriyaki; and a very special Katsura moriawase. Flavours are delicate. Presentation is gorgeous by a knowing service staff outfitted in the traditional kimono. ❦ The international list of well-known wines is probably one of the most reasonable and complete you'll find among Japanese restaurants.

AVERAGE DINNER FOR TWO: $75
Does not include wine, tax and gratuity.

PACIFIC RIM

Proprietor & Chef	General Manager
MARK MCEWAN	TAREK ABOUSHAKKA

NORTH 44°

2537 YONGE ST.
~ Midtown, north of Castlefield ~
TORONTO, ONTARIO
(416) 487-4897

All major credit cards
Dinner Monday to Saturday • Closed for lunch

MENU HIGHLIGHTS

★★★★★

APPETIZERS
MAYAN TOMATO SALAD WITH
GRILLED GARLIC-STUDDED
PORTOBELLO MUSHROOMS •
CHARRED BLUEFIN TUNA WITH
PEPPERCORN CITRUS CRUST

MAIN COURSES
PAN-FRIED GNOCCHI WITH
SWEET POTATO SAUCE AND
GRILLED GRAIN-FED QUAILS •
GRILLED BLACK GROUPER WITH
BUTTERED SPINACH, TOMATO,
CORIANDER RELISH, CURRY
COCONUT BROTH AND PLANTAIN
CHIPS • ROASTED VEAL
TENDERLOIN WITH WINTER
RISOTTO, GRILLED RADICCHIO
AND OYSTER MUSHROOMS

TOPPING THE SHORT LIST OF "IN" SENSATION:
is North 44° (named for the city's latitude), a lavish dinin
event sophisticated patrons have been heard rhapsodizin
about for days after experiencing it. ❦ Inspiration of Mar
McEwan of Pronto fame, North 44° is an airy, ultra-lux
attitude in a fabulous triple-tiered showcase of glass
copper, tile, carved broadloom, live piano, tallback chair
and meticulous table settings. Two levels of dining room
(both with good perspectives on the glamorous, well
dressed action) languish beneath the popular third-leve
bar. But there is much more to North 44°'s success tha
innovative design. ❦ McEwan's menus resonate with
quality and delight with the unpredictable. Resist, if yo
can, the temptation to satisfy your appetite with th
ravishing appetizers and jalapeño cornbread; the mai
courses (peppered veal punctated with oysters; grille
chicken with satiny risotto) are often occasions in them
selves. Fanciful desserts provide a glossy finish. ❦ Th
service staff, despite the demands intrinsic in such
popular spot, extends itself with charm. ❦ North 44°
uniquely offbeat character extends to the wine list, ric
with international selections by the bottle and glass.

AVERAGE DINNER FOR TWO: $8
Does not include wine, tax and gratuit

INTERNATIONAL FRENCH

OPUS

37 PRINCE ARTHUR ST.
~ Yorkville area, near Park Plaza Hotel ~
TORONTO, ONTARIO
(416) 921-3105

Proprietors
TONY AND MARIO AMARO

Chef
DIDIER LEROY

All major credit cards
Dinner Monday to Sunday • Closed for lunch

MENU HIGHLIGHTS

★★★★★

APPETIZERS
TERRINE OF FOIE GRAS WITH CROUTONS SERVED WITH WARM DUCK GLAZE • SMOKED RAINBOW TROUT MOUSSE WRAPPED IN SMOKED SALMON, SERVED WITH WASABI SOUR CREAM

MAIN COURSES
RED SNAPPER WITH A RED WINE SAUCE AND JULIENNE OF BRAISED ENDIVE • ROASTED RACK OF LAMB WITH A NATURAL JUS AND GARLIC CREAM • PHEASANT ROASTED WITH FRESH CRANBERRY SAUCE AND BLACK PLUMS

NOT YET TWO YEARS OLD, OPUS HAS ALREADY achieved popular and critical acclaim as a chic, romantic, very special Toronto dining experience (no small task in this demanding city!). ❦ Soft, elegant room tones enhance the accomplished cuisine of Chef Didier Leroy in an intimate dining room beautifully dressed for just 60. Service is impeccable, the wine list is remarkably complete, and the location is at the city's fashionable heart. ❦ Under the expert, hands-on direction of owners Tony and Mario Amaro, both of whom have earned their stripes as restaurateurs, the Opus focus is on excellence sans pretention and it accomplishes this easily. ❦ Known for his unforgettable sauces and glazes, an unwavering devotion to freshness and perfect presentation, Chef Leroy's cooking, from appetizers to desserts, is bright with invention and balance. Smoky soups, lacy salads, unusually exciting vegetables; perfectly grilled and roasted meat, fish and fowl; and velvety homemade pastas both lusty and delicate, star on menus never allowed to tire. ❦ An exceptional international wine collection favours French with a pleasing Californian and Italian presentation. ❦ Summer patio.

AVERAGE DINNER FOR TWO: $65
Does not include wine, tax and gratuity.

ORSO

106 JOHN ST.
~ Theatre District, near Skydome ~
TORONTO, ONTARIO
(416) 596-1989

All major credit cards
Dinner Monday to Sunday • Lunch Monday to Friday

Proprietor
JOHN MAXWELL

MENU HIGHLIGHTS

★★★★★

APPETIZER
VENISON TENDERLOIN
CARPACCIO WITH ARUGULA,
CELERY, EXTRA-VIRGIN OLIVE
OIL & LEMON

MAIN COURSES
CARTA MUSICA: WAFER-THIN
PIZZA WITH GARLIC, EXTRA-
VIRGIN OLIVE OIL & ROSEMARY
• CALF'S LIVER SAUTÉED WITH
ONION, BALSAMIC VINEGAR &
THYME • GRILLED ATLANTIC
SALMON WITH BLACK OLIVE
BUTTER, ARTICHOKE & TOMATO

DESSERT
BERRIES MARINATED IN GRAND
MARNIER WITH GOAT'S MILK
ICE CREAM

THERE ARE TWO INVITING SUMMER TERRACES here: one on the rooftop of Orso's dignified, two-storey, 19th-century venue; the other, in back. Inside, two dining levels brim with easy sophistication and gentle Italian ambiance. The simple, softly pastel decor whispers class with wooded floors, pale marble walls, and smiling, expert service. Personal photos of Italy and friends of owner, John Maxwell, entertain the eye. Exciting the palate, however, is where Orso really excels. ❦ Hot, parchment-thin pizza bread drizzled with rosemary-tinged olive oil goes well with aperitifs and menu ruminations. Offerings begin with a serious list of luscious appetizers, the best wafer-thin crust designer pizzas in town, and enlivened pastas. Representing all (rather than just a region) of Italy, courses then lead to such features as Grilled Marlin, Striploin with Shiitake Mushroom and Barolo; lamb, veal and sublime chicken dishes served with snapping fresh vegetables. There are no wrong choices from Chef Mano's kitchen. ❦ The exclusive cellar is comprised largely of privately imported Italian finds. A pair of small bars on each floor serve cocktails, wine by the glass, beer, a variety of grappas and cappuccino.

AVERAGE DINNER FOR TWO: $75
Does not include wine, tax and gratuity.

CHINESE/SZECHUAN

Hosts
STANLEY KWAN
CHARLES YEUNG

Dim Sum Chef
KWOK FOON MAK
Executive Chef
KAM TONG KWONG

PEARL HARBOURFRONT

207 QUEEN'S QUAY WEST
~ Queen's Quay Terminal upstairs, near York St. ~
TORONTO, ONTARIO
(416) 203-1233

All major credit cards
Dinner and Lunch Monday to Sunday

MENU HIGHLIGHTS

★★★★★

APPETIZERS
DEEP-FRIED CRAB CLAWS
• DEEP-FRIED SPINACH WITH WALNUTS

MAIN COURSES
LEMON CHICKEN • LOBSTER
WITH NOODLES IN SUPREME
SAUCE • RAINBOW CHOP IN
CRYSTAL FOLD

DESSERTS
DEEP-FRIED ICE CREAM
• MANGO PUDDING

THE SLEEK PEARL HARBOURFRONT HAS BEEN at home for 10 years in this glossy, multi-windowed, second-storey waterfront location-with-a-view. ✿ For the past eight years, this restaurant has been among *EnRoute Magazine's Top 100* (selected by reader's choice). In 1992, two of the restaurant's four partners, Kam Tong Kwong (Executive Chef) and Kwok Foon Mak (Dim Sum Chef), captured honours at the *First World Competition of Chinese Cuisine* held in Shanghai. And it was Pearl Harbourfront the Hong Kong government sought out to prepare dinner for 1,200 visitors. ✿ Hospitable hosts Stanley Kwan and Charles Yeung, behind Pearl Harbourfront's success, have reason to be proud of their informed, well turned-out service staff. ✿ Dim Sum is a luncheon standout here, or, day or night, order from the à la carte menu which features no fewer than 20 house specialties. Vietnamese-Style Beef on Hot Iron Plate and Chicken Cubes in Phoenix Nest are high-demand favourites. ✿ *Management has recently opened a second location: Pearl Yorkville, 110 Bloor Street West. Telephone (416) 975-1155.*

AVERAGE DINNER FOR TWO: $60
Does not include wine, tax and gratuity.

Proprietor
MICHAEL E. CARLEVALE

Chef
MASSIMO CAPRA
Maître d'
FERNANDO TEMUDO

PREGO DELLA PIAZZA

150 BLOOR ST. WEST
~ Downtown, Yorkville area ~
TORONTO, ONTARIO
(416) 920-9900

*All major credit cards
Dinner and Lunch Monday to Saturday*

MENU HIGHLIGHTS

★★★★★

APPETIZERS
MIXED FRESH VEGETABLE
ANTIPASTO • CARPACCIO DI
FILETTO • CALAMARI FRITTI

MAIN COURSES
HAND-MADE RAVIOLI
• SPAGHETTI WITH
FINGER-CHOPPED VEGETABLES
• BLACK ANGUS SIRLOIN
• PIZZA-OVEN ROASTED CHICKEN
• GIANT SEA SCALLOPS
• SEA BASS

DESSERT
TIRAMISU

WHEN TORONTO FIRST WOKE UP TO FINE
Italian cuisine in the late '70s, congenial Michael Carlevale
was there with funky Carlevale's on Avenue Road which,
during the late '80s, grew up to become Prego Della
Piazza, a bright, sophisticated, confident restaurant/bistro
(with a summer piazza behind the lovely old Church of the
Redeemer) in slick Yorkville. ❦ Tremendously popular
and extremely friendly, Prego showcases both a formal
dining room and a more casual "bistro" side, both impec-
cably decorated. With seating for 140, plus, in season, 60
on the patio, reservations are recommended and celebrity
peeking is often rewarding. ❦ For four years, Chef Massimo
Capra's accomplished preparation and presentation has
continued to draw patrons and reviewers back for more.
Inventive salads; delectably grilled and seasoned market
fresh vegetables; grilled fish and fowl; and splendid
sautéed pastas all shine. ❦ The service staff nears perfection in its hospitality, accommodation and knowledge. ❦
The outstanding wine collection (many by the glass)
underlines Italian vintners with a good Pacific Northwest
selection and some choice international vintages.

AVERAGE DINNER FOR TWO: $7.
Does not include wine, tax and gratuity

CONTINENTAL

THE ROOF

4 AVENUE ROAD
~ Park Plaza Hotel, Yorkville district at Bloor ~
TORONTO, ONTARIO
(416) 924-5471

All major credit cards
Dinner Monday to Sunday • Closed for lunch

Executive Sous-Chef
DERECK ALLEN
Corporate Executive Chef
DOMINIQUE DIEN
Restaurant Chef
MICHAEL SULLIVAN

Restaurant/Lounge Manager
SERGE CAMBOU
Maître d'
TONY COSTA

MENU HIGHLIGHTS

★★★★★

APPETIZERS
LOBSTER AND TRUFFLE RAVIOLI,
VANILLA AND CHAMPAGNE
BEURRE BLANC • WARM
ASPARAGUS AND WILD
MUSHROOM TART • HEART OF
BOSTON SALAD (GORGONZOLA,
APPLE AND PECANS)

MAIN COURSES
GARLIC RACK OF LAMB,
SEMOLINA GNOCCHI •
BROCHETTE OF SCALLOPS,
CRISPY EGG NOODLES IN A
BLACK BEAN SAUCE • POACHED
ATLANTIC HALIBUT, CARROT
AND SUNFLOWER OIL, PURPLE
RISOTTO

"WE'VE BEEN DAZZLED WITH FOOD, WINE AND service beyond our expectations ..." says the *Financial Post*, "...could any gourmand fail to be impressed?" ✾ Toronto sophisticates have long regarded "the Roof of the Park Plaza" as the city's premier meeting place. Today, still with the most spectacular downtown view of all, this traditional venue rising from the heart of glossy Yorkville is home to the refined, relaxed Roof Restaurant, deservedly honoured twice in the past two years with *CAA 4-Diamond Awards*. ✾ Intimate, elegant dining is seamlessly orchestrated by Host and Manager, Serge Cambou, his skill honed in France, in the private employ of the Rothschild family. The quiet service is impeccable; the presentation, picture-perfect. ✾ Lyon-born Chef, Dominique Dien's superbly innovative Table d'Hôte and Prix Fixè menus "would be considered exciting in any of the world's great eating cities ...". ✾ As one might expect of a restaurant of this calibre, the wine collection is outstanding with aperitifs and champagne by the glass offered from the trolley. ✾ Cocktails and nightcaps are also served with grace in the adjacent fireside lounge-with-a-view.

AVERAGE DINNER FOR TWO: $80
Does not include wine, tax and gratuity.

ROPPONGI

230 RICHMOND ST. WEST
~ Downtown, one block west of University Ave. ~
TORONTO, ONTARIO
(416) 977-6622

Proprietor	Manager
ATHENA HO	PAUL LI

All major credit cards
Dinner Monday to Sunday • Lunch Monday to Friday

MENU HIGHLIGHTS

★★★★★

APPETIZERS
ROPPONGI PLATTER (CHOICE OF 3
FROM A SELECTION INCLUDING
MARINATED BEEF SLICES, SQUID
WITH SPICY SZECHUAN SAUCE,
SHREDDED CHICKEN WITH
CUCUMBER & AGAR AGAR, ETC.) •
SHARK'S FIN SOUP WITH CRABMEAT
• HOT AND SOUR SOUP

MAIN COURSES
DICED CHICKEN WITH SZECHUAN
GARLIC SAUCE • MOO-SHU BEEF
SERVED WITH PANCAKES • FRIED
SCALLOPS, SHRIMP AND SQUID •
PEKING DUCK (THREE COURSES) •
SHREDDED PORK WITH CUCUMBER
• MEAT DUMPLINGS IN BAMBOO
STEAMER (DIM SUM SELECTION)

IN TOKYO, THE NAME ROPPONGI IDENTIFIES
particular upmarket area. In Toronto, Roppongi is a soft
sophisticated dining room well worth remembering whe
the palate yearns for oriental delicacies brilliantly pr
pared and exquisitely presented. ❦ You are not likely
"stumble" upon this restaurant. It resides in an unlikel
looking building apart from the restaurant area. Insid
sensitive lighting dramatizes a rich grey room adorne
with a fascination of unusual brushed aluminum, bra
and copper tabletops softened by deep, cushy banquette
❦ Szechuan cooking is the specialty here, although mar
Cantonese choices appear on the Chef's menus. A mode
selection of appetizers precedes an impressive array
seafood, beef, chicken, duck and pork dishes. "No d
scription could do justice to 'Goldfish swimming in
pond'...such a beautiful rendition of shrimp and veget
bles is rarely seen outside of the Orient" says the *Financi
Post*. ❦ Owner, Athena Ho, commands a smart, accom
modating staff (some of whom speak Japanese). Th
international wine list, although limited, is carefully ar
well chosen. ❦ At 10 p.m., guests take the spotlight for
karaoke songfest.

AVERAGE DINNER FOR TWO: $:
Does not include wine, tax and gratui

SCARAMOUCHE
RESTAURANT • PASTA BAR & GRILL
1 BENVENUTO PLACE
~ West of Avenue Rd., south of St. Clair Ave. W. ~
TORONTO, ONTARIO
(416) 961-8011

All major credit cards
Dinner Monday to Saturday • Closed for lunch

General Manager	Chef de Cuisine
CARL KORTE	KEITH FROGGETT

MENU HIGHLIGHTS

★★★★★

APPETIZERS
LOBSTER AND SPINACH
SAUSAGE • WARM SWEETBREAD
AND WILD MUSHROOM TERRINE
• FENNEL MARINATED ATLANTIC
SALMON

MAIN COURSES
HICKORY SMOKED AND GRILLED
ATLANTIC SALMON • PAN
ROASTED RIESLING MARINATED
QUAILS • SEAFOOD MEDLEY IN A
SAFFRON NAGE • PEPPER ROASTED
RACK OF LAMB • GRILLED ROWE
FARM FILET MIGNON

DESSERTS
HAZELNUT BOMBE WITH WARM
SABAYON • COCONUT CREAM PIE

ONE BENVENUTO PLACE IS A PRESTIGIOUS downtown apartment address, distinguished even more by the presence there of Scaramouche, a dining room classic by any standards. ❦ Overlooking the glitter of downtown from a wonderful hillside setting, Scaramouche (acclaimed by Toronto patrons in 1993 as their number one favourite), holds great attraction to the cognoscenti. ❦ Soft, subtle and decidedly romantic, the premises-with-a-view is divided into the formal restaurant and a discreet pasta bar with a wide array of light dishes and tender pastas (the formal dining room's wine list and dessert menu are also offered here). ❦ Executive Chef, Keith Froggett, is the master behind the menus, ably assisted by Sous-Chefs Boban Mathew and Lisa Nicholson. Complex tastes, skillfully understated, seem married by nature. Fish and seafood dishes are of particular note. Presentation is showcase-perfect. Pastry Chef Joanne Yolles's desserts are legendary. ❦ Flawless service is executed by an elite staff of thorough professionals. ❦ Wines (including a number of Grand Crus) are carefully chosen and represent many nations. ❦ Scaramouche also offers cooking classes in the kitchen studio led by Chef Instructor Kevin McKeachie.

AVERAGE DINNER FOR TWO: $80
Does not include wine, tax and gratuity.

Food and Beverage Director
BILL LESLIE

Executive Chef
HAROLD FOO

TOP OF TORONTO
REVOLVING RESTAURANT

~ CN TOWER ~
301 FRONT ST. WEST
TORONTO, ONTARIO
(416) 362-5411

All major credit cards
Dinner Mon. to Sun. • Lunch Mon. to Fri. (Brunch Sat. & Sun.)

MENU HIGHLIGHTS

★★★★★

APPETIZERS
WILD MUSHROOMS WITH
MADEIRA AND PORTO GLAZE •
BAKED WOOLWICH GOAT CHEESE,
ROASTED SWEET PEPPERS AND
BALSAMIC TOMATOES

MAIN COURSES
GRILLED GIANT SHRIMP WITH EGG
TAGLIALINI AND BASIL PESTO •
FRESH ATLANTIC SWORDFISH
WITH OYSTER MUSHROOMS AND
LEMON CITRUS BUTTER •
CANADIAN ANGUS BEEF
TENDERLOIN WITH CABERNET
STILTON SAUCE

DESSERT
MANDARINE MOUSSELINE WITH
CREAM CITRUS BUTTER

ONE HUNDRED AND FOURTEEN FLOORS ABOVE Toronto, Top of Toronto Revolving Restaurant, located in the CN Tower, has the most breathtaking views of the city. ❦ For leisurely lunch and dinner meals, enjoy the classically prepared dishes of Executive Chef Harold Foo. Dedicated to introducing new and contemporary menus, Chef Foo and his team favour local fare and have lightened the cuisine with such products as Canadian Angus beef, Ontario lamb, Brome Lake duckling and New Brunswick Atlantic salmon. Considerable attention is given to creating a style that is simple, modern and always memorable. For dessert, a sampling from the sumptuous dessert menu is a must. ❦ Complementing Top of Toronto's exquisite cuisine is Food and Beverage Director Bill Leslie's ongoing *MasterChef Showcase* program which features the culinary signature of a different world-class Toronto Chef each month. ❦ The majority of wines on the effusive international wine list are private imports with Canada well represented. A generous selection is available by the glass.

66

AVERAGE DINNER FOR TWO: $70
Does not include wine, tax and gratuity.

TRUFFLES

21 AVENUE ROAD
~ In the Four Seasons Hotel, Yorkville district ~
TORONTO, ONTARIO
(416) 928-7331

Hotel General Manager	Executive Chef	*All major credit cards*
KLAUS TENTER	DENIS JARICOT	*Dinner Monday to Saturday*

MENU HIGHLIGHTS

★★★★★

APPETIZERS
SMOKED APPLEWOOD SALMON
• SPAGHETTINI WITH BLACK
TRUFFLES • WILD FIELD
MUSHROOMS AND ASPARAGUS
RAGOUT

MAIN COURSES
SAUTÉED ATLANTIC SALMON
WITH VEGETABLE FETTUCCINI
• ROAST RACK OF LAMB WITH
PROVENCE HERBS AND
VEGETABLE • ROAST QUEBEC
DUCK WITH MARINATED ORANGE
AND CELERY ROOT PURÉE •
VEAL TENDERLOIN WITH
CREAMED MUSHROOMS AND A
MOREL SAUCE

TRUFFLES ECLIPSES ITS STATUS AS A HOTEL dining room to stand alone among all of Toronto's restaurants as, most agree, the queen of them all. Laden with honours, Truffles, in 1993, became the first and only Canadian ever to number among the *World's 10 Great Hotel Restaurants.* Yet Truffles is as unlike a hotel restaurant as a great dining room can be. ❦ Totally transformed after a glorious redesign, Truffles reopened in April '93 to thunderous ovations by press and patrons for its airy, grandly sophisticated design enlightened with a dash of whimsy; and applause for the artful culinary expressions of Executive Chef Denis Jaricot. ❦ Traditional French cooking techniques in concert with the intense, robust nature of local and regional ingredients result in haunting, sunny, herb-fragrant flavours that smack unmistakably of Provence. Appetizers are amazing. Salads, inspired. The definitive Grilled Swordfish is just one of the menu choices. Desserts by Pastry Chef Paulette Sanchez are works of art. ❦ Internationally accredited Sommelier, Christophe Le Chatton, manages Truffles and commands the fabulous collection of wines, an impressive selection of which is available by the glass.

67

AVERAGE DINNER FOR TWO: $85
Does not include wine, tax and gratuity.

CONTINENTAL

Executive Chef
DOMINIQUE DIEN
Sous-Chef
NOEL FERNANDEZ

Maître d'
EMILIO CALDERON

ZACHARY'S

950 DIXON ROAD
~ In The Bristol Place Hotel,
near Pearson International Airport ~
TORONTO (REXDALE), ONTARIO
(416) 675-9444

All major credit cards
Dinner Mon. to Sat. • Lunch Mon. to Fri. (Brunch Sun.)

MENU HIGHLIGHTS

★★★★★

APPETIZERS
ZACHARY'S LOBSTER BISQUE
WITH XO ARMAGNAC AND
CIRSPY CELERIAC • STILTON AND
SMOKED HAM FRITTERS, SHAVED
FENNEL AND WILD BERRIES •
CHARRED SEA SCALLOPS

MAIN COURSES
ROAST VENISON MEDALLIONS,
TANQUERAY GIN AND SHALLOT
MARMELADE • GREEN RISOTTO
SERVED WITH SHRIMPS,
SCALLOPS, SOLE AND SALMON •
GRILLED ATLANTIC SALMON ON
SAUTÉED SPINACH WITH SALFSIFI
AND CHERVIL RAGOUT

NEITHER YOUR NAME NOR YOUR WISHES are overlooked at Zachary's, for 21 years a Bristol Place Hotel attraction to businesspeople, celebrations and out-of-town visitors. ❦ Early-evening piano stylings, low ceilings and deep, quiet colours lend something of a "supper-club" aura to the handsome room for 110 guests. ❦ Zachary's smiles with congenial service by a long-tenure staff overseen by personable Emilio Calderon, Maître d'Hôtel for 15 years. ❦ French Chef Dominique Dien and Sous-Chef Noel Fernandez combine imagination with tradition to create original menus that change bi-monthly. Seared Alligator Fillets; Roasted Rack of Lamb crusted with garlic and rosemary; and fresh Dover Sole are house specialties. ❦ The complete wine list features over 200 international entries. ❦ For a spectacular sampler of this kitchen's capabilities, try Sunday Brunch. ❦ Chef Dien often works with guests to plan exclusive dinners (complete with a printed commemorative menu) for private groups.

AVERAGE DINNER FOR TWO: $50
Does not include wine, tax and gratuity

BEAVER CLUB

900 RENÉ LÉVESQUE BLVD. WEST
~ Queen Elizabeth Hotel ~
MONTREAL, QUEBEC
(514) 861-3511

Maître d'	Executive Chef
CHARLES PLOEM	JEAN K. CORDEAUX

All major credit cards
Dinner Mon. to Sun. • Lunch Mon. to Fri.
(Brunch Sun.)

MENU HIGHLIGHTS
★★★★★

APPETIZERS
LOBSTER VOL-AU-VENT WITH
BLACK MORELS • SCAMPI SOUP
WITH CAVIAR & SAUTERNES

MAIN COURSES
SHRIMP, SALMON & SCALLOP
BOUILLABAISSE • GRILLED PINK
TUNA STEAK WITH MARINATED
GINGER • N.Y. PEPPERED
BEAVER CLUB SIRLOIN
"MAÎTRE CHARLES" • GRILLED
DUCKLING WITH FIVE
PEPPERCORNS

DESSERTS
CRÊPES SUZETTE • WARM
CHOCOLATE TARTS WITH
ORANGE & MORELLO
CHERRY SAUCE

IT HAS BEEN SAID THAT IF THE WALLS OF THE Beaver Club could talk, E.F. Hutton would listen. Powerful regulars hold court here, and the handsome room with its rich, private hunting club lustre is a well-suited accommodation. ❦ Subtly refined in 1992, the Beaver Club's unique, historic character was carefully preserved in fine carved wood, tasteful appointments and historic mementos. ❦ Charles Ploem, for over three decades the room's distinguished host, melds his expertise with that of Chef Jean K. Cordeaux and a devoted service staff to capture an old-world grace rarely found today. ❦ With total reverence for the traditional values of French haute cuisine, Chef Cordeaux lends invention to his already remarkable menus with inspired Asian and Californian touches. The luncheon table d'hôte notes facts for the diet conscious, but at night meals are a bountiful celebration presented with great style and panache. ❦ French wines dominate the fine, expansive cellar and Sommelier Jean-François Tournet's particular pride in the Beaver Club's private, peerless vintage collection is well justified.

AVERAGE DINNER FOR TWO: $75
Does not include wine, tax and gratuity.

BOMBAY PALACE

2051 St. Catherine St. West
~ Downtown ~
Montreal, Quebec
(514) 932-7141

All major credit cards
Dinner and Lunch Monday to Sunday

Proprietor
Iqbal Chatwal

Menu Highlights

★★★★★

APPETIZERS
Onion Bhajia
• Assorted platter

MAIN COURSES
Butter chicken • Lamb
chops Khandahari
• Seafood vindallo
• Sali boti • Palace
sizzling grill

DESSERTS
Ras malai •
Gulab jaman
• Mango ice cream

FOR OVER 20 YEARS NOW, BOMBAY PALACE has been a trusted favourite among Montreal's knowledgeable university crowd, who still refer to it as the Pique-Assiette. Now modernized and redecorated, Bombay Palace has retained its traditional cozy atmosphere while adding style and flair to its long-proven recipe for success. ❧ Under the thoughtful direction of Owner Iqbal Chatwal, this restaurant has earned wide popular appeal and a vast loyal following. Regulars range from the younger folk who appreciate early-bird specials and high-quality dining, to the more mature and genteel clientele who recognize excellence when they taste it and refined ambiance when they feel it. Service staff is helpful; the large, easy-to-read menus appreciated. ❧ A gorgeous selection of mouthwatering, oven-baked tandoori entrées caters to the faint of tongue: no overly-hot surprises here. In addition, a special menu of low-cholesterol dishes appeals to the health-conscious. ❧ At Bombay Palace, every menu item is a savory adventure and every sauce, from angelic to devilish, a royal delight. ❧ *Bombay Palace's second location in the Montreal area: 3343 Boulevard des Sources, Dollard des Ormeaux (Tel. 685-3263).*

AVERAGE DINNER FOR TWO: $35
Does not include wine, tax and gratuity.

BONAPARTE

443 RUE ST. FRANÇOIS XAVIER
~ Old Montreal ~
MONTREAL, QUEBEC
(514) 844-4368

Proprietor
LOUIS LADOUCEUR

Chef
NICOLAS CARRERE
Manager
ALAN RIENDEAU

All major credit cards
Dinner Monday to Sunday • Lunch Monday to Friday

MENU HIGHLIGHTS

★★★★★

APPETIZERS
LOBSTER BISQUE SEASONED WITH
GINGER • SAUTÉED SNAILS IN FILO
WITH CREAMY PESTO SAUCE •
SHRIMP RAVIOLIS WITH LEEK AND
SOYA BUTTER SAUCE

MAIN COURSES
BRAISED TUNA STEAK WITH
MUSHROOMS IN VERMOUTH SAUCE
• LOBSTER MEDALLIONS POACHED
IN VANILLA SAUCE WITH FRESH
SPINACH • ROASTED RACK OF
LAMB IN PORT SAUCE AND
VEGETABLES À LA PROVENÇALE
• TORNEDOS OF VENISON IN A
BITTER CHOCOLATE SAUCE

DESSERTS
DELICATE WARM APPLE PIE •
GRAND MARNIER SOUFFLÉ

IN THE SHADOW OF THE FAMED NOTRE DAME Basilica's spires, next to The Centaur, the city's premier English language theater, is sequestered this exquisite gem of a restaurant whose name honours the Emperor and whose classic yet contemporary cuisine honours all who appreciate superior dining. ❦ Under Manager Alan Riendeau, Bonaparte's often surprising menu includes table d'hôte choices for lunch or dinner. Chef Nicolas Carrere describes his eye-pleasing cuisine as "moderately modern, happily classic, never boring," created to satisfy a wide spectrum of tastes. ❦ Seating just 69, each table is quietly illuminated, its floating, flowered centrepiece delicately spotlit. Above the central dining room and the glass-enclosed atrium terrace — appropriately named La Serre — secluded balconies overlook the Old Montreal street scene, providing dining intimacy ideal for cloistered meetings or romantic tête-à-têtes. Service is subdued, stylish and discreet. ❦ The primarily French wine list is best described as "complete." And when it comes time to linger over coffee and dessert, several superior vintage ports await, adding the perfect finishing touch to the Bonaparte experience.

AVERAGE DINNER FOR TWO: $65
Does not include wine, tax and gratuity.

Chef
MATTEO YACOUB

Co-Proprietor
MAX LECAS

BUONA NOTTE

3518 ST. LAURENT
~ The Main, north of Sherbrooke St. ~
MONTREAL, QUEBEC
(514) 848-0644

All major credit cards
Dinner Monday to Sunday • Lunch Monday to Friday

MENU HIGHLIGHTS

★★★★★

APPETIZERS
FUNGHI ALLA GENOVESE CON POLENTA • CACCIATORE CON CAPRINO • RISOTTO GIARDINIERA • CARPACCIO BUONANOTTE • PIZZA AI FUNGHI

MAIN COURSES
FISH OF THE DAY (MAHI-MAHI, GROUPER, SWORDFISH) • INVOLTINI DI POLLO AL "BAROLO" • ALASKA KING CRAB WITH BLACK FUSILLI • BLACK RAVIOLI STUFFED WITH LOBSTER MEAT AND SALMON

LOCATED ON TRENDY AND ECLECTIC ST. Laurent Boulevard (otherwise known as "The Main"), Buona Notte gives the impression of a private cocktail party where dinner is also being served. The crowd is a fascinating collection of exuberant young Montrealers and visitors, many of whom are regulars. As the evening progresses, often well into the morning, the "joie de vivre" runs high. The atmosphere is casual and lively, with the sound of contemporary tunes at a level the young demand and appreciate. ❦ In addition to offering many designer pizzas, fresh and interesting pastas, and the regular menu, ever-present and convivial Chef Matteo Yacoub lists his "specials of the evening" (both appetizers and table d'hôte items, which change twice daily) on a well-placed blackboard. Food is fresh and of consistently high standards while remaining moderately priced. ❦ The room is generally crowded, with little space to maneuver among the closely-arranged tables — yet mysteriously, the youthful, energetic staff manage to provide deft and proficient service. ❦ The compact wine list includes a well-chosen selection of mostly Italian wines, along with a few very good Californian choices. ❦ Buona Notte's bars, the Horseshoe Bar and adjoining one, are ideal for mingling.

AVERAGE DINNER FOR TWO: $55
Does not include wine, tax and gratuity.

CAFÉ DE PARIS

1228 SHERBROOKE ST. WEST
~ Ritz-Carlton Kempinski Montreal ~
MONTREAL, QUEBEC
(514) 842-4212

Hotel General Manager
RENÉ GOUNEL

Maître d'
HENRI JULIEN
Executive Chef
MICHEL LANOT

All major credit cards
Dinner Mon. to Sun. • Lunch Mon. to Sat.
(Brunch Sun.)

MENU HIGHLIGHTS

★★★★★

APPETIZERS
ATLANTIC SALMON SMOKED AT
THE RITZ • RÖSTI OF SNAILS IN
A PASTRY & PESTO CREAM
SAUCE • FRESH BELUGA CAVIAR

MAIN COURSES
FEUILLETÉ OF SALMON À LA
RITZ • SAUTÉED CALF'S LIVER
WITH PICKLED GINGER &
TARRAGON • AIGUILLETTES OF
MAGRET OF DUCKLING, MAPLE
CARAMEL SAUCE WITH STAR
ANIS

DESSERTS
TIMBALE OF BERRIES & FRUITS
IN SEASON • CHESTNUT
CHARLOTTE

HARDLY A CAFÉ, THIS, THE SIGNATURE DINING room of Montreal's richly distinguished Ritz-Carlton Kempinski Montreal Hotel, is an elegant old-world aristocrat in handsome shades of blue and gold. ❦ Flawless tables dressed with lamps, flowers and gleaming settings are sensitively attended under the watchful eye of Maître d', Henri Julien. Service is discreet, impeccable. ❦ The elegant drawing-room ambiance is a splendid setting for the inspired dégustation, table d'hôte, and à la carte presentations of Chef Michel Lanot who describes his cuisine as "evolutive" rather than classic French, preferring *au jus* to cream and butter as the base for a repertoire of sauces capable of faithful authenticity and great enhancement. Very light, low sodium dishes are noted on the menu. ❦ Accredited Sommelier, Jean-Pierre Gaudin, presides over a vast wine cellar representative of every important wine region of the world. ❦ *In appropriate weather, the room's French doors open onto the famous, romantic Jardin du Ritz ("country garden" complete with duck pond), a seasonal "must", particularly for the Sunday Brunch Gastronomique. Note the Ritz Bar (cocktails) and Le Grand Prix piano bar (dancing).*

AVERAGE DINNER FOR TWO: $75
Does not include wine, tax and gratuity.

LE CHANDELIER

825 CÔTE VERTU ROAD
~ 10 minutes north of Downtown ~
MONTREAL (ST. LAURENT), QUEBEC
(514) 748-5800

Proprietors	General Manager	*All major credit cards*
DICK AND FRANCINE	ANDRÉ BOYER	*Dinner Monday to Sunday • Lunch Monday to Friday*
MACKAY		

MENU HIGHLIGHTS

★★★★★

APPETIZERS
GOAT CHEESE AND MUSHROOM
MOUSSE • SCALLOPS WITH SUN-
DRIED TOMATOES AND BASIL •
WARM SHRIMP SALAD À LA
RASPBERRY VINAIGRETTE

MAIN COURSES
RACK OF LAMB WITH HERBS
PROVENÇALES AND ONION CONFIT
• SLICED BREAST OF DUCKLING
SERVED WITH GRAND VENEUR
SAUCE • GRILLED LOBSTER TAILS
WITH PINK BUTTER

DESSERTS
CHOCOLATE PRALINE CAKE •
STRAWBERRY MOUSSE CAKE WITH
FRESH FRUIT • TROPICAL HOUSE
SHERBET

THE VENERABLE HOME OF LE CHANDELIER, with its two-foot thick fieldstone walls and wood-burning fireplaces, dormer windows and original hand-hewn beams, has survived more than two centuries on today's eclectic Côte Vertu. ❦ Nurtured by Dick and Francine MacKay, the graciously relaxed setting exudes welcome and enduring dignity. Soaring walls showcase Francine's own Quebec countryside paintings, 18th century domestic artifacts and festive copper. Here you'll find a textured environment, warmed by ladderback chairs, antique pine and creative table dressings. An appealing loft "library" provides seating with a bird's-eye view of the main dining room. The charming, private Salon Grou is a favourite for business or family gatherings. In all, 125 guests may be accommodated. ❦ Cuisine is an enlightened version of French Classic, interpreted in a light, innovative style. Delectable à la carte, table d'hôte and dégustation offerings feature seasonal specialties expertly prepared with the freshest the market has to offer at realistic prices. ❦ Wines are well-chosen, primarily French and selected Californians, with a good choice in half-bottles or by the glass. ❦ A "find".

AVERAGE DINNER FOR TWO: $6
Does not include wine, tax and gratuity

LES CHENÊTS

2075 BISHOP STREET
~ Downtown ~
MONTREAL, QUEBEC
(514) 844-1842

Sous-Chef MAGALIE GILLET Chef & Proprietor MICHEL GILLET	Maître d' JOSÉ PARRA Hostess SYLVIE GILLET

All major credit cards
Dinner Monday to Sunday • Lunch Monday to Friday

MENU HIGHLIGHTS

★★★★★

APPETIZERS
MEDALLION OF FOIE GRAS WITH
TRUFFLES • SEAFOOD IN PASTRY •
LOBSTER THERMIDOR • SALMON
WITH WHITE BUTTER SAUCE

MAIN COURSES
BEEF FILET WELLINGTON
• SALMON AND HALIBUT
COMBINATION • RACK OF LAMB
PROVENÇAL • SUPREME OF DUCK
IN COINTREAU SAUCE • ESCALOPE
OF VEAL "ANGEVINE"

DESSERTS
CHEESEBOARD • SYMPHONY LES
CHENÊTS • RASPBERRY SABAYON
• VIRGIN KISS • PROFITEROLES
WITH CHOCOLATE SAUCE

FOR 20 YEARS, THIS MULTI AWARD-WINNING, family-run restaurant has served as an oasis of fine French dining to celebrities, food connaisseurs, Montrealers and visitors alike. ❦ French-born Chef/Owner Michel Gillet, along with his daughters, Sous-Chef Magalie and Hostess Sylvie, strive to make the Les Chenêts experience memorable from the moment their guests step through the door. ❦ Muted colours; the soft glow of burnished copper pots, pans and skillets; fresh-cut flowers; monogrammed tableware; tablecloths and napkins edged in lace: all contribute to the elegance and sophistication of this very special place. ❦ Service, led by Maître d' José Parra, is polished, formal and always professional. ❦ Acknowledged on numerous occasions by *Wine Spectator* as home to Montreal's most impressive and notable collection of French wines, Les Chenêts offers 35,000 bottles representing 2,800 labels in every price range. ❦ After dinner, select from one of the 180 Cognacs or 120 ports as a befitting finale to an unforgettable dining experience. ❦ *Immediately below the restaurant, the Bistro du Musée serves lunch from the same kitchen. Excellent value.*

AVERAGE DINNER FOR TWO: $75
Does not include wine, tax and gratuity.

CANTONESE/SZECHUAN

General Manager
RAYMOND ST. PIERRE

Executive Chef
KEN CHONG

CHEZ CHINE

99 VIGER AVENUE WEST
~ In the Holiday Inn Centre-ville
Jardin Sinomonde, Chinatown ~
MONTREAL, QUEBEC
(514) 878-9888

All major credit cards
Dinner, Lunch & Dim Sum Monday to Sunday

MENU HIGHLIGHTS

★★★★★

APPETIZERS
BIRD'S NEST SOUP WITH HAM AND
CHICKEN • STEAMED SHARK'S FIN
DUMPLING IN A SOUP • BAMBOO
FUNGUS STUFFED WITH SHRIMP
PASTE • DEEP-FRIED STUFFED
CRAB CLAWS • SHREDDED ROAST
DUCK WITH FRESH FRUITS

MAIN COURSES
LIVE LOBSTER SAUTEED IN OIL •
CRISPY SHREDDED BEEF
SZECHUAN STYLE • BAKED
BROWNS WITH SPICY SALT AND
CHILI • "MU SHUI" OF PORK
ROLLED A PANCAKE • DEEP-FRIED
FILET OF CHICKEN, FRESH LEMON
SAUCE • TRADITIONAL ROAST
DUCK PEKING STYLE

HERE IS WHERE THOSE WHO KNOW THE difference come for Cantonese food as it should be. As one of Montreal's finest, authentic Chinese restaurants, the food does live up to its magnificent surroundings. ❦ Located in the hotel opposite the Montreal Convention Centre, its central location, with indoor parking, is on the edge of Chinatown and within a stone's throw of Notre Dame Basilica in Old Montreal. The dining room replicates a Chinese garden, and the luxuriousness of space creates an oasis of tranquility with miniature lakes replete with fish; pagodas; trees and plants; waterfalls and fountains; and an atrium exposing open skies above. ❦ Presided over by Executive Chef Ken Chong, the menu offers over 150 authentic choices in all, including shark's fin specialties, famous Peking duck, vegetarian dishes, many dishes representing various regions of China, and a month-watering parade of 30 Dim Sum specialties prepared by Dim Sum Chef Liang Yudong and served fresh from the kitchen rather than cold from the cart at lunch every day of the week. ❦ The wine list, although primarily French, does offer some interesting selections from California, Australia, Chile, and even an interesting Chardonnay from China. ❦ Led by Maître d'Hôtel, Barry Lau, the knowledgeable service staff is friendly and accommodating.

AVERAGE DINNER FOR TWO: $60
Does not include wine, tax and gratuity.

CHEZ LA MÈRE MICHEL

1209 GUY ST.
~ Between St. Catherine & René Lévesque W. ~
MONTREAL, QUEBEC
(514) 934-0473

Chef & Proprietor
MICHELINE DELBUGUET

Maître d's
MARC RAFANELLI
AMERICO SILVA

All major credit cards
Dinner Mon. to Sat. • Lunch Tues. to Fri.

MENU HIGHLIGHTS
★★★★★

APPETIZERS
ASPARAGUS & SWEETBREAD
IN PUFF PASTRY • LIGHT &
FLUFFY ONION PIE
• MÈRE MICHEL
BOUILLABAISSE • BELLY FISH
TURNOVER WITH BASIL
BUTTER

MAIN COURSES
LOBSTER SOUFFLÉ NANTUA •
RABBIT IN MUSTARD SAUCE •
FRESH VEAL KIDNEY FLAMBÉ
• VEAL, BEEF & LAMB
MEDALLIONS WITH THREE
SAUCES

LIKE A CHERISHED OLD FRIEND, CHEZ LA MÈRE Michel is very special, very lovely. ❦ The enchanting country atmosphere enhanced by rustic wooden beams, weathered copper artifacts, and expert tuxedoed service brims with warmth and grace. There's a charming atrium here; and downstairs the low-ceilinged "wine cellar" (complete with archways, aged wine bottles and Henry VIII seating) provides a third very special setting. ❦ Winner of the *Gastronomie Quebecoise Award,* co-owner Micheline Delbuguet (herself distinguished as *Best Female Chef* by Salon de La Femme) has, for 25 years, remained faithful to her menu of delectable specialties from all the regions of France. ❦ Hailing from a Côte d'Azure restaurant family, Madame Delbuguet, who has been practicing culinary artistry all of her life, insists on farm-fresh ingredients, and goes herself to her sources to ensure the very best. ❦ Seasonal highlights are available and vary daily. ❦ The flattering wine list is extensive, primarily French, and realistically priced.

AVERAGE DINNER FOR TWO: $70
Does not include wine, tax and gratuity.

FRENCH

Host & Proprietor
PAUL DAHAN

Chef Cuisinier
NICOLAS JONGLEUX

LE CINTRA

2072 DRUMMOND
~ Downtown, south of Sherbrooke St. ~
MONTREAL, QUEBEC
(514) 284-2132

All major credit cards
Dinner Monday to Sunday • Lunch Monday to Friday

MENU HIGHLIGHTS

★★★★★

MAIN COURSES
DUCK LIVER WITH SPICED APPLE
JELLY • ARCTIC CHAR WITH
NUTS AND LEMON JUICE •
YOGURT RAVIOLE WITH CURRIED
LANGOUSTINES AND CUCUMBER •
LOBSTER TOURNEDOS IN CHICK
PEA PANIS, SERVED WITH
CANDIED TOMATOES • GRILLED
DOUBLE VEAL CHOP • LAMB
ROULADE À LA MUSCADE •
DUCK FOIE GRAS PAVÉ WITH
LENTIL CONFIT AU BALSAMICO

DESSERTS
WARM CHOCOLATE TOURTE
• ANISEED ICED PARFAIT

IN 1993, ACCOMPLISHED RESTAURATEUR PAUL Dahan introduced to Montreal his new partner, Nicolas Jongleux, trained and experienced in the kitchens at two Michelin-rated, three-star restaurants in France: Alain Chapel's in Lyons and (as first chef) at George Blanc's in Vonnas. ❦ Now, thoroughly enjoying Montreal with its marvellous markets, the youthful Chef Jongleux goes shopping each morning to personally ensure that every morsel offered on the day's menu — including the sinfully scrumptious desserts — will be the very best and the very freshest. One mark of his personal pride and culinary confidence is the Menu de Dégustation: a series of surprise courses individually created to the delectation of delighted diners. ❦ Host Dahan presides with pride over the dining room, classically decorated in warm harvest tones, and the airy and more informal atrium garden patio. Service is thoroughly professional and attentive to every need, making the entire experience an idyllic choice for those who wish to dine in true French style, whether on a limited or unlimited budget. ❦ The wines, decanted at tableside for serving, represent all major French regions plus a smattering of Italian and Californian, several available by the glass. ❦ Le Cintra's popular bar offers an impressive selection of 65 brands of single malt whiskies and 45 Cognacs to be savoured before and/or after dining.

AVERAGE DINNER FOR TWO: $70
Does not include wine, tax and gratuity

LES CONTINENTS

360 SAINT ANTOINE STREET WEST
~ In the Hotel Inter-Continental Montreal,
Old Montreal ~
MONTREAL, QUEBEC
(514) 987-9900

Sommelier & Maître d'
STÉPHANE LORTIE
Manager
PIERRE JULLIEN

Executive Chef
JACKY FRANÇOIS

All major credit cards
Dinner Mon. to Sun. • Lunch Mon. to Sat. (Brunch Sun.)

MENU HIGHLIGHTS

★★★★★

APPETIZERS
SYMPHONY OF THREE SALMONS,
SUN-DRIED CRANBERRY SAUCE •
CLAM CHOWDER WITH CURRY •
DUCK CONFIT, SPINACH AND WILD
MUSHROOMS IN A SPRING ROLL
SHEET

MAIN COURSES
SALMON, FLAVOURED WITH
MIRIN, IN ITS NORI SHEET, HONEY
DILL SAUCE • LOIN OF LAMB,
CAJUN-STYLE MUSTARD,
CROUSTIL OF GUACAMOLE •
THINLY-SLICED, ROASTED WAPITI
WITH A PEPPERCORN AND JUNIPER
BERRY SAUCE

DESSERT
POACHED PEARS WITH HONEY
SABAYON

JUST OVER THREE YEARS OLD, THE TASTEFULLY appointed fine dining room of Montreal's newest luxury hotel is already attracting both a local business crowd and international visitors to Chef Jacky François' eclectic southwestern, oriental and Cajun artistry. Inspiration comes directly from the market; emphasis is on freshness and creativity; and menu variety is often dazzling. ❦ Always a pleasant surprise, each evening's table d'hôte features a different country: Piccata of Salmon and "Yamaimo Soba" with Sesame Seeds one night may be replaced by Duck Breast, "Yucatan" flavours the next, then perhaps something French. À la carte and dégustation menus are equally attractive and widely varied. Cajun-style chicken breast on a bed of Caesar salad; marinated vegetables in a crispy rice shell; tempura of the day; and Mediterranean hors d'oeuvres are popular selections. In the evening, three types of fresh fish are prepared in the style of your liking. ❦ Maître d' and national award-winning Sommelier, Stéphane Lortie, presents an international list of wines showing a slight partiality toward California vineyards. The vast majority of selections are available by the glass. ❦ Service, led by Manager Pierre Jullien, is sincere, professional and attentive.

79

AVERAGE DINNER FOR TWO: $70
Does not include wine, tax and gratuity.

LES HALLES

1450 CRESCENT ST.
~ Between de Maisonneuve West & St. Catherine ~
MONTREAL, QUEBEC
(514) 844-2328

Proprietors
JACQUES & ITA
LANDURIE

Chef
DOMINIQUE CRÉVOISIER

All major credit cards
Dinner Mon. to Sat. • Lunch Tues. to Fri.

MENU HIGHLIGHTS

★★★★★

APPETIZERS
SALMON AND LOBSTER TERRINE
• GRAPEFRUIT MARIE-LOUISE

MAIN COURSES
STUFFED SALMON WITH GREEN
PEPPER SAUCE • LOBSTER AUX
HERBES AND LIGHT BUTTER
SAUCE • QUAIL WITH SOUR
CHERRIES • GUINEA HEN WITH
RED CABBAGE

DESSERTS
TATIN PIE • ST. HONORÉ
• PARIS BREST

ENQUIRE ABOUT
"SURPRISE DU PATRON"
GASTRONOMICAL MENU

LES HALLES IS A SEAMLESS, SENSUOUS "MUST
for afficionados of the art of fine dining. ❦ During its 2?
year history in the century-old greystone, honours hav
been heaped upon Les Halles, the most recent the covete
Le Trophé Ulysse crowning this Montreal's finest gou
met restaurant by people's choice. ❦ Themed after the Ol
Market in Paris, Les Halles has recently undergone
joyful rejuvenation which, with fresh, happy colours ar
natural light, has brought the enchanting cachet to lif
Chef Dominique Crévoisier, a member of owners Jacque
and Ita Landurie's Les Halles family for 13 years, maste
fully captures the new, lighter attitude in many of h
inspired creations. ❦ Luncheon has evolved into a Car
de Midi with special wines available. Evening men
include a Table d'Hôte Gourmande which changes se:
sonally, a Table d'Hôte du Jour, a Gastrono-mique "Su
prise du Patron," and breathtaking à la carte selections.
A formidable cellar complements the cuisine with 3(
predominantly French wines. The lustrous service is e:
emplary.

AVERAGE DINNER FOR TWO: $8
Does not include wine, tax and gratui

Chef
NOBERT LENNARTZ

Maître d'
LUIGI BOCCIA

LA MARÉE

404 PLACE JACQUES-CARTIER
~ Old Montreal, corner rue St-Paul ~
MONTREAL, QUEBEC
(514) 861-8126 • 861-9794

All major credit cards
Dinner Monday to Sunday
Lunch Monday to Friday

MENU HIGHLIGHTS

★★★★★

APPETIZERS
SEAFOOD SALAD
• LOBSTER BISQUE

MAIN COURSES
FILETS OF SOLE WITH
CHAMPAGNE • MEDITERRANEAN
SEA BASS • SAUTÉED LOBSTER
WITH TOMATO & BASIL •
HALIBUT FILET WITH FOIE GRAS
• VEAL MEDALLIONS WITH
ORANGE SAUCE • ROASTED
BREAST OF DUCK

DESSERTS
SELECTION OF OUR CHEF'S
HOMEMADE CREATIONS

LIKE ANTIQUE COGNAC, LA MARÉE'S REFINED elegance deserves to be savored slowly. ❦ Beyond the appealing entrance display of pâtés, terrines and other hints of the gastronomic delights in store, a wash of pearl gray and burgundy harmonizes softly with the glossy patina of old wood and shimmering napery in the seductive light of this ancient stone dwelling in Old Montreal. Three aristocratic rooms accommodate up to 90 discerning guests in generous, upholstered luxury at tables discreetly placed for privacy. ❦ Chef Nobert Lennartz's presentations are a tribute to classic French cuisine with memorable French sea bass, lobster, game birds, veal, lamb and beef specialties. Sauces are lavish. Desserts, homemade and indulgent. ❦ Repeatedly honoured with CAA's *Four Diamond Award (1992 and 1993)*, of particular note is La Marée's talent for *guéridon* (cart) service which privileges guests to the masterful tableside preparation of their choices by skillful waiters with a genuine talent for performance. ❦ For 19 years, partner and Maître d', Luigi Boccia, has ensured a seamless dining experience which has proven especially attractive to the sophisticated epicurean.

AVERAGE DINNER FOR TWO: $85
Does not include wine, tax and gratuity.

Manager
ABDO ABOUHAMAD

Chef
HELMUT TSCHERNE

LA MER

1065 PAPINEAU AVE.
~ South of René-Lévesque Blvd. East ~
MONTREAL, QUEBEC
(514) 522-2889

All major credit cards
Dinner and Lunch Monday to Sunday

MENU HIGHLIGHTS

★★★★★

APPETIZERS
BELUGA CAVIAR • SMOKED
STURGEON • SMOKED ARCTIC
CHAR • SQUID AND OCTOPUS
SALAD • LOBSTER BISQUE •
NOVA SCOTIA CLAM CHOWDER •
FRIED SQUID • FRESH OYSTERS
OR CHERRYSTONE CLAMS

MAIN COURSES
POACHED SALMON WITH
CHAMPAGNE SAUCE •
CHARBROILED HALIBUT WITH
BÉARNAISE SAUCE • MAHI MAHI
WITH GINGER • FLAMBÉED
SWORDFISH WITH PEPPER SAUCE
• FRIED SOFT-SHELLED CRABS •
STEAMED OR GRILLED LOBSTER
• FILET MIGNON

IN MONTREAL, THE NEXT BEST THING TO A restaurant at an oceanside fishing pier is found minutes from downtown, at La Mer. ❦ Housing a fish market, this two-tiered fish and seafood emporium offers four distinct dining choices. On the lower level, there's the Sushi Bar; Moules & Cie., a casual dining adventure featuring the "catch of the day"; and the Mediterranean, marine-themed Agora Room, where fish of your choice is grilled simply and to perfection, Greek psarotavernas-style. ❦ On the upper level is the signature dining room, where Austrian-born, Swiss-trained Chef Helmut Tscherne offers every imaginable treatment of the fresh fish and seafood found in La Mer's own market. ❦ Soft candlelight, a fireplace setting, and the soothing sounds of the room's waterfall centrepiece are ideal for a romantic evening. Window-side tables come with a view of the Jacques Cartier bridge, which connects the island of Montreal to the mainland. ❦ Service, under the very capable direction of Manager Abdo Abouhamad, is professional and knowledgeable. ❦ The well-chosen wine list is primarily white and French, and offers a generous selection of half-bottles. ❦ *Music to dance by on Friday and Saturday evenings.*

AVERAGE DINNER FOR TWO: $50
Does not include wine, tax and gratuity.

GREEK

Proprietor
COSTAS SPILIADIS

MILOS' STAFF

MILOS

5357 AVE. DU PARC
~ North of rue Laurier ~
MONTREAL, QUEBEC
(514) 272-3522

All major credit cards
Dinner Mon. to Sun.
Lunch Mon. to Fri. & Sun.

MENU HIGHLIGHTS

★★★★★

APPETIZERS
GRILLED MEDITERRANEAN
OCTOPUS WITH CAPERS
• MILOS SPECIAL
(EGGPLANT, ZUCCHINI,
SAGANAKI, TZATZIKI)

MAIN COURSES
DEEP-SEA NOVA SCOTIA
LOBSTER (3 - 25 LBS. EACH)
• CHARCOALED AMERICAN
RED SNAPPER •
CHARCOALED SWORDFISH
STEAK • FRESH QUEBEC
LAMB CHOPS • FRESH
DOVER SOLE

OWNER COSTAS SPILIADIS HAS FAULTLESSLY honed Milos into an international word-of-mouth attraction where the bottom line is excellence, pure and simple. ❦ The modest storefront opens into a dynamic environment that fairly shimmers with taste and cheerful energy, wrapped in a decor aptly described as "a marriage of humble and elegant". First impressions come in waves: an open-air market; a tiny Greek village; a glossy Aegean villa. ❦ Glass showcases burdened with perfect vegetables and market-crisp fruit compete for attention, while Milos' renowned Mediterranean bass, red snapper, Dover sole, Arctic char, stone crabs, pompano, barbouni and other gifts from the seas of choice rest clear-eyed on crushed ice, fresh enough to blink. ❦ Festive checked tables happily accommodate 200 in a room where fame rubs shoulders with 14-year devotees, and Costas' watchful eye misses nothing. ❦ Few require a menu, all expect perfection without fanciful adornment, and Costas makes it his business to ensure no guest is ever disappointed. ❦ Newcomers can't make a wrong choice. Don't overlook the oyster mushrooms, octopus, charcoaled shrimp, and a world-class tzatziki.

AVERAGE DINNER FOR TWO: $80
Does not include wine, tax and gratuity.

STEAKS & FRESH FISH

Proprietors
LARRY & LENNY LIGHTER

General Managers
HY COGAN &
TONY CAMACHO

MOISHES

3961 BLVD. ST. LAURENT
~ Between Pine & Duluth Avenues ~
MONTREAL, QUEBEC
(514) 845-3509

All major credit cards
Dinner Mon. to Sun. • Lunch Mon. to Sun.

MENU HIGHLIGHTS

★★★★★

APPETIZERS
PICKLED SALMON • SHRIMP
COCKTAIL

MAIN COURSES
CHARCOAL-BROILED STEAKS
• CHARCOAL-BROILED FRESH
FISH • CHARCOAL-BROILED
VEAL & LAMB CHOPS
• CHARCOAL-BROILED
CHICKEN

DESSERTS
HOMEMADE PASTRIES
• HOMEMADE COOKIES

FIFTY-FIVE YEARS AGO MOISHE OPENED THE doors with a no-nonsense idea of quality, quantity, consistency and good old-fashioned hospitality. Today, under the expert guidance of sons Larry and Lenny Lighter, all these qualities remain intact, excellence prevails and Montreal's premier steak house has taken its rightful place as one of the city's prized traditions. ❦ For 44 years Chef O'dillon Fournier has been firing Moishes' red brand, aged, grain-fed beef to perfection over hardwood charcoal, and continues to overwhelm patrons with 18-ounce rib steaks, 23-ounce T-Bones, outstanding fresh grilled fish, and Moishes' own interpretation of chicken. ❦ Generations of families and celebrity alike come together at well-dressed tables in the single, upholstered, club-like upstairs room suited to the comfortable accommodation of 225. Moishes has entertained everybody from Sinatra, Newman, Olympians and politicians, to the Cardinal who became Pope. ❦ Service is smoothly professional as one might expect of a staff who, in large part, have been part of the Moishes family for decades.

AVERAGE DINNER FOR TWO: $60
Does not include wine, tax and gratuity.

Proprietors
LEO, STEFANO, CHARLIE & LEONARDO
IACONO

LE MUSCADIN

100 ST. PAUL STREET W.
~ Old Montreal, corner St. Sulpice Street ~
MONTREAL, QUEBEC
(514) 842-0588

All major credit cards
Dinner Monday to Saturday • Lunch Monday to Friday

MENU HIGHLIGHTS

★★★★★

APPETIZERS
FANTASIA DI FUNGHI •
ANTIPASTO VEGETARIO
• BRESSAULA MOSCARDINO

MAIN COURSES
LINGUINE CON SEPIA • VITELLO
PORCINELLA • AGNELLO DEI
CONTI-ROMANI • ANITRA
AGRO-DOLCE • FILETTO DI
MANZO ZINGARELLI •
GAMBERONE RICARDO

DESSERTS
TARTUFFO ALLA PANNA •
ZAMBAGIONE CON CANNOLI
SICILIANI

WHILE OLD MONTREAL OFFERS MANY FINE French restaurants, those who prefer classic Italian dining know there's only one choice, and Le Muscadin is it. This pretty restaurant features elegant service by formally attired waiters whose command of the menu is exceeded only by their artistry in tableside presentation. Included in the repertoire: flambéed delights; fresh pasta dishes; and culinary marvels such as Fantasia di Funghi, a blend of three types of seasonal mushrooms that must be savoured to be believed. ❦ Appropriate to its Old Montreal location, Le Muscadin is classically appointed in rich tones of beige and brown, exposed brickwork, fresh-cut flowers and candle-lit tables. ❦ Owned for seven successful years by the Iacono family, two of the four family members, Maître d' Leo and Chef Leonardo, proudly direct Le Muscadin in Old Montreal; two others, Charlie and Stefano, head the second location at St. Sauveur, in the Laurentian mountain resort region. ❦ The wine list is outstanding, with a serious representation from virtually all regions of Italy, major and minor, and a depth of vintages from many eminent houses. More than 10,000 bottles are cellared in state-of-the-art facilities.

AVERAGE DINNER FOR TWO: $65
Does not include wine, tax and gratuity.

Manager & Co-Proprietor
GEORGE LAU

Chef & Co-Proprietor
KWOK-KIT KIU

L'ORCHIDÉE DE CHINE

2017 PEEL STREET
~ Downtown ~
MONTREAL, QUEBEC
(514) 287-1878

All major credit cards
Dinner Monday to Sunday • Lunch Monday to Friday

MENU HIGHLIGHTS

★★★★★

APPETIZERS
AROMATIC CRISPY DUCK WITH
SPRING ONIONS, CUCUMBERS
AND PANCAKES • SESAME
SHRIMP TOAST • RAVIOLI
WITH SESAME SAUCE

MAIN COURSES
STEAMED FISH WITH GINGER
AND SCALLIONS • SLICED
CHICKEN WITH SZECHUAN
PEPPER AND CRISPY SPINACH
• ORANGE-FLAVOURED BEEF
• PEKING-STYLE, SOFT
HOME-MADE NOODLES WITH
VEGETABLES

GEORGE LAU AND FAMILY ARE INTERNATIONALLY renowned for their superior Szechuan cuisine, first introduced in their two fine Montreal establishments, L'Orchidée de Chine and the original Le Chrysanthème; and in their Chrysanthème restaurants in Miami's South Beach and in the Laurentians' St. Sauveur. Now, all that experience is proudly displayed at L'Orchidée de Chine, beautifully redecorated at its familiar Peel Street location in the heart of Montreal. ❦ With parking problems eliminated by courteous valet service, arriving guests are greeted by gentle strains of oriental lute music and a special sense of grace and quality that presages an exquisite dining experience. ❦ Seating 180 on three elegant levels, the atmosphere is chic and the decor refined: art deco with subtle touches of texture and muted colour. The tables, set with freshly cut flowers, are works of art. ❦ Service is polished and professional, as waiters in formal black jackets present a succession of innovative Szechuan dishes and the latest in taste delights from trend-leading Chef, Kwok-Kit Kiu. And be assured, the menu is as health-conscious as it is sensually appealing.

AVERAGE DINNER FOR TWO: $50
Does not include wine, tax and gratuity.

LE PARIS

1812 STE-CATHERINE WEST
~ Downtown, just west of rue St-Mathieu ~
MONTREAL, QUEBEC
(514) 937-4898

Proprietor	Chef
GUY POUCANT	ROBERT BONICARD

All major credit cards
Dinner Monday to Saturday
Lunch Monday to Saturday

MENU HIGHLIGHTS

★★★★★

APPETIZERS
BRANDADE DE MORU (SALTED COD NIMOISE) • MAQUEREAU FRAIS AU VIN BLANC (FRESH MACKEREL IN WHITE WINE) • SOUPE A L'OIGNON GRATINÉE

MAIN COURSES
FOIE DE VEAU MEUNIÈRE (PAN-FRIED CALF'S LIVER) • SAUMON FRAIS POCHÉ, BEURRE BLANC (FRESH SALMON, POACHED, WITH WHITE BUTTER) • ENTRECÔTE BORDELAISE (SIRLOIN BORDELAISE) • RIS DE VEAU SAUTÉS (SAUTÉED SWEETBREADS)

DINERS CHARMED BY THE UNPRETENTIOUS, inexpensive, populated bistros of Paris are certain to be charmed by Le Paris. This is as friendly a restaurant as can be found; a local secret; a word-of-mouth success overflowing with habitués. ❦ For 37 years, owner and manager Guy Poucant and his wife Marie-Claude, with their unfailingly excellent French Bourgeoise cuisine and warm informality, have quietly attracted myriad dévotees who insist "It's like eating at home, only better". ❦ Le Paris is authentic, dynamic, with waiting lines most of the time; yet small and soft enough that the close quarters and swirling energy contribute positively to its convivial character. ❦ Home-cooked dishes are as hearty as they are subtle. Unwavering popularity has dictated the menu remain virtually unchanged, and so it has, since the restaurant's 1956 debut. ❦ The staff have no "stations" here, nor are they in uniform. Everyone, including the Poucants, pitches in everywhere. The performance of service is friendly, homey, and rapid. ❦ Many good wines are available by the glass from the ample, primarily French, wine list.

AVERAGE DINNER FOR TWO: $40
Does not include wine, tax and gratuity.

FRENCH (PROVENÇAL)

LE PETIT LOGIS

2065 BISHOP STREET
~ Downtown ~
MONTREAL, QUEBEC
(514) 987-9586

Proprietors and Hosts
BOBBY AND GLORIA BOUZOUITA

Chef
DAVID BERMUDEZ

All major credit cards
Dinner Monday to Sunday • Lunch Monday to Friday

MENU HIGHLIGHTS

★★★★★

APPETIZERS

SOUPE DE POISSONS À LA ROUILLE
• CALMARS FRAIS SAUTÉS
SAUCE TOMATE AUX HERBES ET
CUMIN • SARDINES FRAÎCHES À
L'ESCABÈCHE

MAIN COURSES

BOURRIDE À LA PROVENÇALE
• AGNEAU FRAIS AU CAVIAR
D'AUBERGINES, HERBES ET AIL •
SAUMON BRAISÉ AUX ÉPINARDS
ET SIROP D'ÉRABLE • FRICASSÉE
DE LA FERME AUX OLIVES,
MOUTARDE ET ROMARIN

DESSERTS

MIRROIR AUX FRUITS EXOTIQUES
• NOUGAT STANKÉ AUX
PISTACHES • VACHERIN MIMOSA

SAID ONE OF THE CITY'S LEADING RESTAUR-ant critics in 1992: " Le Petit Logis wins my vote for the coziest, most intimate little French restaurants with the best food this year." And this restaurant has continued to grow in confidence and appeal. ❦ Outstanding traditional French cooking, with a distinctive accent on the Mediter-ranean and Provence, is the forté here. It is prepared with love by Chef David Bermudez (from Monaco), whose passion for freshness and unmistakable skill for lightness are trademarks. ❦ Veterans of the Montreal restaurant scene for some 22 years, ever-present Owners Bobby and Gloria Bouzouita have attracted a faithful following and tend to their 50-seat, below street-level establishment as they would to invited guests in their home. ❦ The service staff are alert and highly professional — and most obliging in explaining and translating the menu. The decor is tasteful, with candlelit tables, fresh flowers and lace tablecloths set amidst shades of burgundy and grey. ❦ Prices are very fair for a restaurant of this calibre, and the carefully-selected French wine list is a happy complement to the consistently fine cuisine.

AVERAGE DINNER FOR TWO: $55
Does not include wine, tax and gratuity.

Chef/Proprietor
LOUIS NAUD

Hostess/Proprietor
LISE NAUD

LA RAPIÈRE

1490 STANLEY ST.
~ Downtown ~
MONTREAL, QUEBEC
(514) 844-8920

All major credit cards
Dinner Mon. to Sat. • Lunch Mon. to Fri.
(Closed July)

MENU HIGHLIGHTS

★★★★★

APPETIZERS
RILLETES D'OIE
• JAMBON DE BAYONNE

MAIN COURSES
CONFIT DE CANARD AU
VINAIGRE FRAMBOISE
• CONFIT D'OIE
• CARRÉ D'AGNEAU RÔTI
AUX HERBES

ENQUIRE ABOUT
"LA CUISINE DU MARCHÉ"
(TABLE D'HÔTE SELECTION OF
THE CHEF'S MARKET-FRESH
CREATIONS)

FOR ALMOST 20 YEARS, UNASSUMING LA Rapière has been delighting downtown patrons with menu specialties faithful to the Pyrénées region of southwest France. ❦ Goose Cassoulet, Confit of Duck with Raspberry Sauce, Bayonne-style Ham, Veal Sweetbread with Morels, and Rack of Lamb are among the hearty bourgeois favourites relished here by former Prime Ministers and locals alike. ❦ Ever-present owners Louis and Lise Naud were the first to introduce the wines of southwest France to Montreal, and while the 100-choice list bears serious looking-into, it is the authentic à la carte and table d'hôte menu options that keep bringing guests back for more. ❦ Ladderback chairs for 85 and homespun wooden tables dressed in fine linen cozy into two casual rooms warmed with creamy stucco walls, timber trim and friendly touches one might find in a home hidden in the French countryside. ❦ This is an informal, warmly hospitable little family-run restaurant with a fine, far-reaching reputation built on consistent excellence.

AVERAGE DINNER FOR TWO: $55
Does not include wine, tax and gratuity.

Proprietors
FRANKIE CHAN AND JOYCE PANG

SAWATDEE

3453 NOTRE DAME ST. WEST
~ West of Atwater, one block from Atwater Market ~
MONTREAL, QUEBEC
(514) 938-8188

American Express and Mastercard
Dinner Monday to Sunday • Lunch Monday to Friday

MENU HIGHLIGHTS
★★★★★

APPETIZERS
KOUNG CHAE NAAM PLAA (RAW
SHRIMP WITH SALT FISH SAUCE
AND MINT LEAVES) • TOM YAM
KOUNG (HOT AND SOUR SHRIMP
SOUP WITH LEMONGRASS) • YAM
NEUA (BEEF SALAD WITH ONION,
HOT CHILI AND MINT LEAVES

MAIN COURSES
CHOO CHI KOUNG (SAUTÉED
SHRIMPS WITH SPICY SAUCE) •
TA-LAY PAD KRA PLOW (FRESH
SEAFOOD WITH HOT CHILI AND
SWEET BASIL LEAVES) • GAENG
PED GAI (CHICKEN IN GREEN
CURRY, COCONUT MILK AND BASIL
LEAVES) • PHANAENG NEUA
(SAUTÉED BEEF IN RED CURRY
AND COCONUT MILK)

ABOUT A DECADE AGO, WHEN THAI CUISINE
swept the nation as the culinary rage of North America,
Montreal was slow off the mark. ❦ Today, with
Sawatdee, Owners Joyce Pang and Frankie Chan have
achieved what a host of others could not: that is, bring
authentic, upscale Thai dining to the city. Here, according
to critical and popular acclaim, is the best Thai
food in Montreal. ❦ The location seems remote from
other dining areas, but, as Joyce points out, parking is
a breeze. ❦ Once inside Sawatdee, you're whisked into
an oriental underworld of Thai artifacts, art treasures,
tapestries and museum pieces. The service staff (in
beautifully bejewelled vests) expertly tends three tiers
softly drenched in pink, gray, burgundy and antique
rose. The food is superb; the choices staggering. Come
with a large party, if you can, to sample a more
expansive array of the available dishes. ❦ Sawatdee's
cooks, schooled by an esteemed Thai chef whom Joyce
brings in for occasional "refresher" courses, have
learned their lesson well. Dishes range from authentically
blazing to warmly seductive, depending upon
your taste. Soups are exceptional; salads, outstanding;
curries, unusually memorable. ❦ Be sure to reserve.

AVERAGE DINNER FOR TWO: $4
Does not include wine, tax and gratuity

LA SILA

2040 St. Denis
~ Latin Quarter ~
MONTREAL, QUEBEC
(514) 844-5083

Proprietors	Maître d'
LUIGI DIGESO	ANTONIO CANDIDO
GINO DIGIOVANNI	Chef
	LUCIO CIPRIANO

All major credit cards
Dinner Mon. to Sat. • Lunch Mon. to Fri.

MENU HIGHLIGHTS

★★★★★

APPETIZERS
LOBSTER RAVIOLINI •
MUSSEL SOUP WITH SAFFRON
• GREEN SPAGHETTI WITH
FRESH SALMON AND CAVIAR

MAIN COURSES
CALF'S LIVER ALLA
VENEZIANA • INVOLTINI
ALLA MILANESE • FRESH
SALMON WITH CHIVES AND
PINK PEPPER

DESSERTS
TIRAMISU LA SILA •
SICILIAN CAKE • CHESTNUT
CAKE WITH CARAMEL SAUCE

OWNERS LUIGI DIGESO AND GINO DIGIOVANNI have expanded upon La Sila's classical Italian cuisine with such evocative innovations as Cold Zabaglione with Berries; Fresh Salmon Poached in White Wine with Chives and Pink Peppercorns; Homemade Lobster Ravioli in Lobster Sauce with Tomato. ❦ The La Sila family cares about its guests, and it shows. Consistent excellence and splendid service coupled with elegant surroundings reminiscent of the Calabria region of Southern Italy have made devotees of locals and out-of-towners alike. ❦ Dating from 1895, the original fieldstone walls merge with exposed brick and light, bright contemporary touches, into four rooms. Recent renovations preserve the delightful sense of intimacy and familiar conviviality that prevails for 90 guests, some of whom occasionally short-cut through the kitchen. ❦ La Sila's excellent wine list is exclusively Italian with a fine selection available by the glass. ❦ A summer terrace puts you ringside for such St. Denis Street festivities as Montreal's jazz and comedy festivals. ❦ Reservations, always recommended, are a must on weekends. ❦ *Free parking available.*

91

AVERAGE DINNER FOR TWO: $60.
Does not include wine, tax and gratuity.

Maître d'
Bruno Raggi

Chef
Dominique Poissant

Le St-Amable

188 Rue St-Amable
~ Old Montreal, near Place Jacques-Cartier ~
Montreal, Quebec
(514) 866-3471

All major credit cards
Dinner Monday to Sunday
Lunch Monday to Friday

Menu Highlights
★★★★★

APPETIZERS
Grilled sea scallops,
oysters, mushrooms, on a
nest of corn salad •
Roasted stuffed quail with
chestnuts & venison, on a
bed of red cabbage

MAIN COURSES
Braised veal cutlet with
scampi, in a mustard seed
sauce • Red mullet filet 'en
croûte' on a purée of sweet
pepper & basil

DESSERTS
Tulip with chocolate
mousse, on a mint-flavoured
custard sauce

IN A CITY THAT TAKES ITS DINING SERIOUSLY, Le St-Amable is an acknowledged classic frequented by locals, sought out by visitors, indulged in by celebrity. ❦ On an artist's lane in Montreal's enchanting Old Quarter, located beneath the street-level French bistro, a fine setting is provided for the award-winning classic French cuisine in a faithfully restored 18th-century stone dwelling, rich with the lustre of old wood and shades of crimson hushed by moody lighting and soothing music. ❦ Maître d' Bruno Raggi takes special interest in the pleasure of his guests which can number up to 60 and often do, particularly during the temperate months. The ambiance is thick with tradition and decidedly romantic. ❦ For eight of Le St-Amable's 26 years, Chef Dominique Poissant has showcased his culinary expertise with such finesse, that changes to the popular à la carte menu are rare and variations of the table d'hôte are offered only every few days. ❦ Service is glossy by seasoned professionals. The complete wine list, dominated by French wines, includes a selection of half-bottles, and a choice of spectacular homemade desserts is also available.

AVERAGE DINNER FOR TWO: $60
Does not include wine, tax and gratuity.

PHOTOS: JEFF LENOIR

Proprietor
CHRISTINE LAMARCHE

Proprietor
NORMAND LAPRISE

TOQUÉ!

3842 RUE ST-DENIS
~ Just north of the Latin Quarter ~
MONTREAL, QUEBEC
(514) 499-2084

All major credit cards
Dinner Monday to Sunday • Closed for lunch
(Group luncheons available by reservation)

MENU HIGHLIGHTS
SAMPLE, WHICH CHANGES DAILY

★★★★★

APPETIZERS
SEARED CALAMARI WITH TOMATO
CONFIT AND RATATOUILLE
GRATINÉ, WITH OLIVE JUS •
SALMON TARTARE WITH AVOCADO
AND CHIVES, SERVED WITH
VEGETABLE CHIPS

MAIN COURSES
SEARED MAGRET OF DUCK WITH
CARAMELIZED KUMQUATS, SERVED
WITH POLENTA OF DRIED FRUIT
AND DUCK CONFIT • HOT
"FRAÎCHEMENT TOQUÉ!"
FOIE GRAS

DESSERT
PURE CARIBBEAN CHOCOLATE
"TURBAN" WITH CARAMELIZED
APPLES

JUST WHEN DINERS WERE BECOMING BLASÉ about the multitudinous choices available to them in Montreal, Toqué! exploded on the scene, setting sleepy critics and patrons aquiver with its daring, exciting contemporary cuisine known as "cuisine du marché." Postmodern Toqué!, with bright chipboard panels and coloured wood floor, has become the current rage, and the kitchen that cooks with such exuberance is the reason. ❦ Sporting avant-garde baseball caps, youthful Owners, Christine Lamarche and Normand Laprise, allow no culinary short-cuts in their open kitchen. Each day's menu is decided by the best the daily market has to offer and the spirited spontaneity of the accomplished Chefs. Anything frozen, be it meat, fish, fowl, vegetables or game, is considered a travesty and isn't allowed through the door. Sauces and stocks are purely enlightened. Desserts are flamboyant and splendid. ❦ English-speaking guests at this refreshing restaurant on stylish St. Denis Street are set totally at ease by a smiling, knowledgeable, bilingual staff who will explain the menu with pleasure. ❦ The wine list is complete and inviting.

AVERAGE DINNER FOR TWO: $60
Does not include wine, tax and gratuity.

FRENCH GASTRONOMY

L'AUBERGADE

53 RUE DRUMMOND
~ Follow signs on Eastern Townships Autoroute ~
GRANBY, QUEBEC
(514) 777-5797

Chef & Co-Proprietor
J. YVES PROD'HOMME

Maître d'
CLAUDE MAURICE

Hostess & Co-Proprietor
AUDREY PROD'HOMME

Visa, Mastercard, Diners Club/enRoute
Dinner Tuesday to Sunday • Lunch Tuesday to Friday

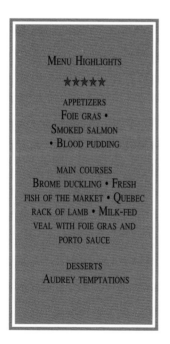

MENU HIGHLIGHTS

★★★★★

APPETIZERS
FOIE GRAS •
SMOKED SALMON
• BLOOD PUDDING

MAIN COURSES
BROME DUCKLING • FRESH
FISH OF THE MARKET • QUEBEC
RACK OF LAMB • MILK-FED
VEAL WITH FOIE GRAS AND
PORTO SAUCE

DESSERTS
AUDREY TEMPTATIONS

AN HOUR AND A QUARTER FROM MONTREAL in the charming town of Granby, visitors and residents alike are drawn to the homespun hospitality of L'Aubergade. Within their fine, more-than-a-century -old Victorian house, Jean Yves and Audrey Prod'homme's delighted customers are treated as welcome guests. Originally from France, Jean Yves is the experienced Chef and Audrey the gracious Hostess. Maître d' Claude Maurice, an integral part of this successful family enterprise since its inception, completes this thoroughly professional knowledgeable team. ❦ L'Aubergade comfortably seats 50 in a small, perfect room decorated in delicate shades of pink and adorned with paintings by local artists. The ambiance of warmth is heightened by copper pans gleaming with reflected candlelight. An adjacent room is available for small, private gatherings. ❦ Most menu items including the foie gras, home-smoked salmon and all pastries, are prepared entirely in L'Aubergade's own kitchen. Each course, separated by a serving of sherbet, is artistically presented to dramatize colour and texture: a true feast for the eyes. ❦ The wine list is very French and very extensive, as befits such a special, small-town place that is well worth discovering.

94

AVERAGE DINNER FOR TWO: $55
Does not include wine, tax and gratuity

CONTEMPORARY REGIONAL FRENCH

AUBERGE HATLEY

350 VIRGIN HILL ROAD
~ Eastern Townships, overlooking Lake Massawippi ~
NORTH HATLEY, QUEBEC
(819) 842-2451

Proprietors
ROBERT AND LILIANE
GAGNON

Chef
ALAIN LABRIE

All major credit cards
Dinner Monday to Sunday

MENU HIGHLIGHTS

★★★★★

APPETIZERS
TERRINE OF FRESH DUCK FOIE
GRAS WITH TRUFFLES • PRAWN
STRUDEL WITH CITRONELLA
BUTTER • SLIVER OF BARBARY
DUCK LEG EN CONFIT AND
ESCALOPE OF FRESH FOIE GRAS

MAIN COURSES
THIN SLICES OF BISON WITH
JUNIPER BERRY SAUCE • STUFFED
FILLET OF BEEF IN "CROÛTE DE
SEL" • SCALLOPS AND PRAWNS
WITH SEAFOOD SAUSAGE AND
WATERCRESS SAUCE

DESSERT
BITTERSWEET CHOCOLATE AND
COFFEE MOUSSE CAKE
WITH FRESH MINT SAUCE

THE ROMANTIC ELEGANCE OF THE LAST CEN-
tury lingers at this Gatsbyesque 1903 country estate
overlooking Lake Massawippi in rural Quebec. ❦
Nurtured by Robert and Liliane Gagnon since 1980
(and listed in the *International Relais & Châteaux
Guide* since 1985), Auberge Hatley was recently honoured as the first in Canada ever to be invited to
perform a dinner at New York's James Beard Founda-
tion, and for the past two years has been awarded the
Table d'Or as the No. 1 restaurant in the province of
Quebec. Even the world-representative wine cellar
was singled out in 1992 with the prestigious *Wine
Spectator Award.* ❦ The exquisite creations of Chef
Alain Labrie arrive at the table like gifts under silver
domes in the graceful, old-world *cloche d'argent* style
of service, which is, of course, flawless. The remarkable cuisine is a joyful marriage of evolutive classic
French and traditional bourgeois, and nobody does it
better. Herbs and salad vegetables come smiling fresh
from Auberge Hatley's own hydroponic greenhouse.❦
The environment is a pure enchantment.

AVERAGE DINNER FOR TWO: $90
Does not include wine, tax and gratuity.

FRENCH

Chef and Co-Proprietor
JACQUES ROBERT
Co-Proprietor
LOUISE DALLAIRE

AU TOURNANT DE LA RIVIÈRE

5070 SALABERRY
~ 20 km east of Montreal, Exit 22
Eastern Townships Autoroute ~
CARIGNAN, QUEBEC
(514) 658-7372

All major credit cards
Dinner Wed. to Sun. • Lunch for private functions only (Brunch Sunday

MENU HIGHLIGHTS

★★★★★

APPETIZERS
TERRINE DE FOIE GRAS •
LANGOUSTINE WITH GINGER
CREAM • SALMON WITH SOYA
SAUCE, AU NOIX ET VERMICELLI
CHINOIS • HALIBUT WITH VIRGIN
OLIVE OIL, HERBS AND TOMATOES

MAIN COURSES
CÔTE DE VEAU WITH WILD
MUSHROOMS AND TARRAGON •
BREAST OF DUCK WITH CONFIT,
PINEAPPLE AND GREEN PEPPER-
CORN • BRAISED DOVER SOLE
WITH FENNEL • LAMB SIRLOIN
WITH ZUCCHINI AND RED PEPPER

DESSERTS
ASSORTMENT OF HOMEMADE
DESSERTS

"THE TURN OF THE RIVER" IS ONE OF THOSE special little secrets insiders like to keep to themselves. Hailed by many as among the nation's finest chefs, Co owner Jacques Robert fell in love with this keepsak country farm 17 years ago. Today, it houses an interio softly brimming with natural light and the airy, upliftin colours of the Mediterranean. Snowy walls galleried with a fascination of original art climb to a ceiling the impos sible colour of the sea. Cushy bamboo armchairs laz around 55 pristine table settings in two discreet, elegantl informal dining rooms, one of which is the irresistibl glass-walled Greenhouse. Chef Robert describes hi signature cuisine as "to my taste." French classic, yes, bu enlightened with a keen sensitivity for the seasons, and delicate touch where inspiration demands. The à la carte table d'hôte and dégustation menus are delectably expan sive, as is your choice of over 250 select wines. Servic is silky, ambiance romantic, homemade desserts wort saving room for. Sunday brunch is served. An idea venue to test your French, but if there are problems, th staff is pleased to assist with explanations of the menu

AVERAGE DINNER FOR TWO: $8
Does not include wine, tax and gratuity

FRENCH

BISTRO À CHAMPLAIN

75 CHEMIN MASSON
~ Exit 69 from Laurentian Autoroute 15 ~
STE-MARGUERITE DU LAC MASSON, QUE.
(514) 228-4988

All major credit cards
Dinner Wednesday to Sunday • Lunch Sunday only

Proprietors	Sous-Chef
MONIQUE NADEAU	CAROLE HALBIG
CHAMPLAIN CHAREST	Chef
	DIDIER GAILDRAUD

MENU HIGHLIGHTS

★★★★★

APPETIZERS
SAUMON FRAIS DE
L'ATLANTIQUE LÉGÈREMENT
FUMÉ • PRESSÉ DE FOIE GRAS DE
CANARD AU NATUREL

MAIN COURSES
MEUNIÈRE DE PÉTONCLES DU
NOUVEAU-BRUNSWICK • FILET
DE TURBOT MARINÉ AUX
AGRUMES • FILET DE BOEUF
GRILLÉ, GRATIN DAUPHINOIS •
MAGRET DE CANARD RÔTI,
DOUX JUS À LA CARDAMOME •
NOISETTES D'AGNEAU POÊLÉ ET
SON JUS AU ROMARIN

DESSERT
CHEESECAKE CHOCOLUTIN •
POIRES ET FRAISES EN SABAYON

OWNER AND HOST, CHAMPLAIN CHAREST, IS A practicing radiologist whose greatest passion is wine. Since meeting, in 1968, the famous French-Canadian artist Jean-Paul Riopelle, and being encouraged to explore the world of wine in greater depth, his outstanding Bistro's assets have come to include what has been called "one of the greatest wine collections in the world": a 25,000 bottle cellar featuring 2,000 selections. Furthermore, apart from the cellar's being awarded the prestigious *Wine Spectator Grand Award* since 1988, the kitchen stands alone, itself a *CAA 4-Diamond Award* winner. ❦ Order à la carte, or partake in Chef Didier Gaildraud's wildly popular six-course menu dégustation which may be accompanied by appropriate wines by the glass. Or, come for the rare experience of foie gras with a '69 Château d'Yquem. Venison and game are often featured on the menu as they are a match to many of the cellar's exceptional vintages. ❦ Set lakeside in an 1864 General Store brimming with antiques and adorned with paintings by Riopelle, this unique restaurant is comfortably casual and informal. ❦ Ask Champlain to show you his cellar; meet gracious Monique Nadeau, Champlain's partner for 12 years; gain an education in wine; indulge in fine food served by waiters who are also sommeliers. The Bistro à Champlain experience is like no other.

AVERAGE DINNER FOR TWO: $80
Does not include wine, tax and gratuity.

Co-Proprietor and Chef
ANNE DESJARDINS
Co-Proprietor and Sommelier
PIERRE AUDETTE

L'EAU À LA BOUCHE

3003 BOUL. STE. ADÈLE
~ 70 km north of Montreal, in the Laurentian Mountains ~
STE. ADÈLE, QUEBEC
(514) 229-2991

All major credit cards
Dinner Monday to Sunday • Lunch Sunday

MENU HIGHLIGHTS

★★★★★

APPETIZERS
CHARTREUSE OF HOUSE-SMOKED
SALMON WITH MUSTARD
CUCUMBERS • MELI-MELO OF
EXOTIC ATLANTIC LOBSTER •
SWEETBREADS WITH
VEGETABLES JULIENNE BRAISED À
L'ANCIENNE

MAIN COURSES
SUPREME OF DUCK IN A PORT
AND APRICOT SAUCE • RACK OF
PIGLET WITH WILD GARLIC • LOIN
OF LAMB IN AN HERBED SAUCE

DESSERTS
MAPLE MOUSSE AND HAZELNUT
CAKE WITH ICE CREAM •
NOUGATINE GLACÉE ON A
RASPBERRY COULIS

IMAGINE! AN IDYLLIC COUNTRY INN. A *Relais & Château* since 1988 in a picturesque Laurentian foothill town less than one hour north of Montreal. Here, talented Chef Anne Desjardins and husband, Pierre Audette, own this renowned restaurant and its adjacent 25-room inn. ❦ Only after earning a degree in Geography did Anne discover her exceptional love and talent for culinary artistry. Her touch is light: just the right herbs and spices for each delicious dish. A recognized leader among today's new breed of Quebec chefs, Anne's efforts have earned glowing reviews in *Country Inns*, *Canadian Living* and France's foremost *Le Figaro*. ❦ Their professionally-trained staff complete an exquisite dining experience in two charming, rustic rooms, each seating about 35. The decor is welcoming, with paintings by local artists, locally-crafted furnishings, soft music, candlelight, and fresh flowers, edible flowers and herbs from their own garden. L'Eau à la Bouche (the name means "mouth-watering") has risen from modest roots to become one of the country's premier restaurants and inns. ❦ The extensive wine list, carefully cultivated by Pierre, is primarily French and fairly priced with a reassuring selection of half-bottles; most important world wine regions are well-represented.

AVERAGE DINNER FOR TWO: $90
Does not include wine, tax and gratuity.

Chef
RÉGIS HERVÉ

AUBERGE DES FALAISES

18 CHEMIN DES FALAISES
~ 90 minutes from Quebec City ~
POINTE-AU-PIC, QUEBEC
(418) 665-3731

All major credit cards
Dinner Monday to Sunday • Lunch Monday to Friday

MENU HIGHLIGHTS

★★★★★

APPETIZERS
PLUS-QUE-PARFAIT DE FOIES DE
CAILLE ET SON SUPRÊME FUMÉ •
TARTIFLETTE DE SAUMON AU
BEURRE DE CURCUMA •
CRÉMEUSE DE CRUSTACÉS AUX
HERBES PANACHÉES

MAIN COURSES
VEAU SAVEUR DE CHARLEVOIX,
SAUCE MOUTARDE DOUCE AU
MIEL "GEMME" • COEUR DE
FILET MIGNON GRILLÉ, COMPOSÉ
DE CHAMPIGNONS SAUVAGES

DESSERT
FONDANT AU CHOCOLAT
MI-CRU, MI-CUIT, GLACE
AU LAIT DE COCO

A SCENIC 90-MINUTE DRIVE FROM QUEBEC City, nestled in the beautiful Charlevoix resort region, the 10-year-old Auberge des Falaises conveys the grandeur of its beginnings as a stately summer residence. ❦ Seating 80 in relaxed elegance, the fine dining room overlooks a forest of cedars, Murray Bay, and the mighty St. Lawrence beyond. Pleasing shades of pink and blue; walls adorned with landscape paintings by local artists; and white wrought iron chairs with deep cushions provide the perfect setting for guests to linger over dinner before adjourning to the equally comfortable lounge. ❦ Thanks to the spreading fame of renowned Chef Régis Hervé (of Tours, France), many arrive for the fabulous menu as well as the fabled view. Chef Hervé's culinary efforts, praised with words such as "fresh" and "harmonious", arrive replete with sauces that both complement the plate and delight the palate. ❦ The wine list represents every wine region of France and includes classics that range from the familiar to the esoteric. True wine connaisseurs will appreciate this fascinating collection, which offers the likes of the rare 1973 Château Petrus Pommerol.

AVERAGE DINNER FOR TWO: $70
Does not include wine, tax and gratuity.

FRENCH

Chef & Co-Proprietor
JEAN MARC BASS

Host & Co-Proprietor
BENITO TERZINI

CAFÉ DE LA PAIX

44 RUE DESJARDINS
~ Old Quebec ~
QUEBEC CITY, QUEBEC
(418) 692-1430

All major credit cards
Dinner Monday to Sunday • Lunch Monday to Saturday

MENU HIGHLIGHTS

★★★★★

APPETIZERS
SCALLOPS WITH CREAM SAUCE IN
PUFF PASTRY • RABBIT WITH
PISTACHIO NUTS TERRINE •
SALMON TARTARE

MAIN COURSES
CARIBOU WITH JUNIPER BERRIES
• SWEETBREADS WITH TRUFFLE
SAUCE • FRESH SALMON WITH
RASPBERRY VINEGAR SAUCE •
VEAL SCALLOPINE WITH MOREL •
TENDERLOIN WITH PEPPER SAUCE
• LOBSTER THERMIDOR

DESSERTS
SABAYON WITH GRAND MARNIER
• CRÊPES SUZETTE

THERE IS MUCH TO BE SAID FOR A RESTAU
rant where the owners are as committed to quality a
they are to "minding the store." And that describes th
style of dynamic, Alsatian-born Chef Jean Marc Bas
and his partner, Host Benito Terzini, who is renowne
for his colourful suspenders and for regaling clientel
with impromptu bursts of song. ❦ After 42 years in th
same ideal location (just minutes from the landmar
Château Frontenac), this handsomely appointed, two
storey establishment, with its romantic Parisian atmos
phere, pastel decor, polished wood and brass, flicker
ing light of hurricane-style lamps on perfectly se
tables, has become a "true Quebec City institution."
Service is knowledgeable, polished and friendly. ❦ A
the adept hands of Chef Bass, culinary traditions ar
perfected without compromise, using only the freshes
of produce and featuring specialties of seafood an
wild game in season. With proper timing, fortunate vis
itors can experience wild caribou or Quebec's famou
salt water lamb. ❦ Primarily French, the wine cella
offers many noble vintages along with a number o
carefully chosen selections from Italy and Californi

AVERAGE DINNER FOR TWO: $6
Does not include wine, tax and gratuity

CLASSICAL FRENCH

LE CHAMPLAIN

1 RUE DES CARRIÈRES
~ Old Quebec, in the Château Frontenac ~
QUEBEC CITY, QUEBEC
(418) 692-3861

All major credit cards
Dinner Tuesday to Saturday • Brunch Sunday
Open every evening May 1st to October 31st

Maître d'hôtel
LOUIS PEREIRA

Chef
ROBERT GAGNON
Executive Chef
JEAN SOULARD

MENU HIGHLIGHTS

★★★★★

APPETIZERS
QUEBEC'S FINEST SMOKED
SALMON • DUCK FOIE GRAS
WITH PRUNES AND ARMAGNAC
JELLY • BUFFALO CONSOMMÉ
WITH STUFFED NOODLES

MAIN COURSES
RACK OF LAMB PROVENÇALE •
DUCK FILLET AND LIVER WITH
SPINACH • FLAMBÉED PEPPER
SIRLOIN STEAK

DESSERT
FLAMBÉED PEPPERED
STRAWBERRIES

INSIDE THE WORLD'S MOST PHOTOGRAPHED hotel, the Château Frontenac, is housed the magnificent Le Champlain. This stately dining room overlooking the St. Lawrence River and the statue of Quebec's founder, Samuel de Champlain, is steeped in Canada's illustrious French heritage. ❦ High expectations are a given in a restaurant of such calibre, and Executive Chef Jean Soulard and Chef Robert Gagnon fulfill them all. Under their expert and enlightened direction, the freshest of ingredients, most obtained locally, marry the flavours of the past with the sophistication of the present. ❦ Service, under the watchful eye of Maître d' Louis Pereira (a 25-year veteran of the Château), is cordial, professional and harmonious. ❦ Staff, outfitted in delightful period costumes, take guests a step back in time. On weekends, the soft tones of harp music further enhance the atmosphere of elegance, grace and history. ❦ The wine list is primarily French; well-chosen to complement the menu; and designed to suit every taste and budget. ❦ *Also recommended: the adjoining Bar St. Laurent, which features a spectacular waterfront view. Ideal for pre-dinner cocktails or after-dinner coffee and digestifs.*

AVERAGE DINNER FOR TWO: $85
Does not include wine, tax and gratuity.

LAURIE RAPHAËL

17 RUE DU SAULT-AU-MATELOT
~ Vieux Port (Old Port) area ~
QUEBEC CITY, QUEBEC
(418) 692-4555

All major credit cards
Dinner Monday to Sunday • Lunch Monday to Friday
(Saturday Brunch summer only; Sunday Brunch year-round)

Chef & Proprietor
DANIEL VEZINA

Hostess & Proprietor
SUZANNE GAGNON

MENU HIGHLIGHTS

★★★★★

APPETIZERS

PORTABELLA CARPACCIO WITH
ROSEMARY AÏOLLI • DUCK
CONFIT LASAGNA WITH FOIE
GRAS AND PORT • OYSTER
TARTARE WITH RUSSIAN CAVIAR

MAIN COURSES

LABRADOR CARIBOU WITH APPLE
CIDER SABAYON • GRILLED RED
SNAPPER, SERVED WITH HEART
OF PALM & RADICCIO SALAD •
LAMB MIXED GRILL WITH
GOAT'S CHEESE AND
TABOULI-FILLED PITA

DESSERTS

MAPLE CRÈME BRULÉE •
MASCARPONE AND COFFEE
CHEESECAKE

WHILE EXPLORING NORTH AMERICA WITH
interludes for serious studies of regional cuisines
Owner/Chef Daniel Vezina and his wife, Partner/Man-
ager Suzanne Gagnon, garnered a host of fresh ideas.
Combining oriental and ethnic with California and
Quebec influences, insight is applied with excellence
and innovation in this intimate restaurant named after
the couple's two children. ❦ The finely-honed talent
of these accomplished restaurateurs become immediately apparent to guests entering one of the two cozy
dining rooms with stone fireplace, or the adjacent patio
courtyard, where the evening sitting is presented al
fresco when the weather co-operates. ❦ Appropriately
the menu is written in French, but the friendly, smiling
and courteous service staff are always ready with
knowledgeable English explanations and recommendations. ❦ Daniel's after-dinner tour of the tables add
an intimate touch to his culinary artistry, including
pastries and desserts, which he personally creates for
up to 60 guests. ❦ The wine list features a wonderful
selection of French and Californian vintages, with a
multitude of choices available by the glass.

AVERAGE DINNER FOR TWO: $60
Does not include wine, tax and gratuity

CONTINENTAL

Executive Chef
DAVID ADAMS

Maître d'
DAVE MCLEAN

GOVERNORS' ROOM

659 QUEEN STREET
~ Downtown, in the Lord Beaverbrook Hotel ~
FREDERICTON, NEW BRUNSWICK
(506) 455-3371

All major credit cards
Dinner Mon. to Sat. • Lunch for private bookings only

MENU HIGHLIGHTS

★★★★★

APPETIZERS
CARPACCIO OF BEEF • BRIE
AND WALNUT PARCELS •
MUSSELS OSCAR • LORD
BEAVERBROOK HOTEL SOUP
(CASHEW NUT AND FENNEL)

MAIN COURSES
NOISETTES OF LAMB •
MIGNOTTES OF BEEF WITH
CHANTERELLE MUSHROOMS •
PAILLARD OF BEEF À LA FAÇON
DU CHEF • TOURNEDOS OF
SALMON WITH TRUFFLES •
FRESH NEW BRUNSWICK
LOBSTER MEDALLIONS,
SCALLOPS AND PRAWNS,
PERFUMED WITH VERMOUTH
AND SAFFRON SAUCE

OVERLOOKING THE SAINT JOHN RIVER IN downtown Fredericton, the respected Lord Beaverbrook Hotel has been earning kudos since Canada's Honourable John B. McNair (later Lieutenant-Governor) laid the cornerstone in 1946. Mere months ago, in late 1993, the Governors' Room opened within this historic Keddy's hotel and in doing so, established itself as Fredericton's premier fine dining room. ❦ The small, classic, club-like Governors' Room (a part of, yet separate from the hotel's more informal Terrace Dining Room) is poshly exclusive with just 14 tables and a maximum capacity of 40 dinner guests. ❦ Fresh fish and seafood are highlights of the well-rounded à la carte menu which includes lamb, beef, pork and fowl. Of particular note are Cordon Bleu Chef David Adams' inventive appetizers and excellent soups (cashew nut and fennel; bisque of lobster with Cognac). Offerings lean toward California and Nouvelle French cuisine in both preparation and presentation. ❦ Maître d' Dave McLean leads a crisply turned-out, friendly and knowledgeable service staff. ❦ The international list offers an eclectic variety of red and white wines (a number of which are available by the glass), and a special Maître d' Selection is suggested.

AVERAGE DINNER FOR TWO: $65
Does not include wine, tax and gratuity.

FRENCH CONTINENTAL

WINDJAMMER

750 MAIN STREET
~ Downtown, in the Hotel Beauséjour ~
MONCTON, NEW BRUNSWICK
(506) 854-4344

Executive Chef
PATRICK BOURACHOT

Maître d'
FRÉDÉRIC MAZEROLLE

All major credit cards
Dinner Monday to Saturday
Available for specialty luncheons on request

MENU HIGHLIGHTS

★★★★★

APPETIZERS
NORTH SHORE MUSSELS IN
WHITE WINE, SHALLOTS, GARLIC
AND LEMON • SPINACH LINGUINE
WITH FRESH SEAFOOD, PESTO
AND TOMATO CREAM • MUSSEL
AND SEAFOOD CHOWDER

MAIN COURSES
ATLANTIC SALMON BAKED WITH
MOROCCAN SPICES, BASIL
MASHED POTATOES AND TOMATO
COMPOTE • ROASTED RACK OF
LAMB WITH HONEY AND
MUSTARD, TURNIP GRATIN •
SAUTÉED BREAST OF GUINEA
FOWL AND TIGER SHRIMP SERVED
WITH CORN POLENTA AND
TARRAGON SAUCE

LUXURIOUS, EXTREMELY INTIMATE AND beautifully attended, The Windjammer *CAA/AAA Four Diamond Award* dining room is itself a special occasion. ❧ The decor's intent is to *"capture the turn-of-the-century opulence of a luxury ocean liner"* in a nautically influenced, 40-seat room elegant with mahogany, fine crystal and upholstered armchairs. ❧ Maître d', Frédéric Mazerolle, believes the key to quality dining is in the detail, and in treating The Windjammer and its guests as though they were his own, sets this apart from less dedicated hotel restaurants. ❧ Chef Patrick Bourachot brings experience from Le Mans in France, the Inn on Lake Manitou, and Toronto's L'Hotel to his confident à la carte and table d'hôte menus. Local seafood specialties (scallops, shrimp, salmon) are often showstoppers; lobster (especially sweet in May) is available May to September; and autumn brings seasonal Indian Summer fish, fowl and game. ❧ Presentation is picture-perfect. Chef Patrick's specialty desserts add a dramatic touch. ❧ The wine list is a complete one, with important international regions represented.

AVERAGE DINNER FOR TWO: $70
Does not include wine, tax and gratuity.

REGIONAL/CONTINENTAL

TURN OF THE TIDE

1 MARKET SQUARE
~ In The Hilton Hotel, adjacent to
Saint John Trade and Convention Centre ~
SAINT JOHN, NEW BRUNSWICK
(506) 693-8484

Executive Chef	Dining Room Manager
MARK J. PERCIVAL	SHIRLEY VAN KRALINGEN

All major credit cards
Dinner Mon. to Sat. • Lunch Mon. to Sun.

MENU HIGHLIGHTS

★★★★★

APPETIZERS
MARITIME SEAFOOD PLATTER
• DIGBY SCALLOP CHOWDER

MAIN COURSES
GRAND MANAN LOBSTERS
• BOUILLABAISSE FOR TWO
• PAN-FRIED SCALLOPS WITH
FIDDLEHEADS AND FIELD
MUSHROOMS IN A VERMOUTH
CREAM SAUCE • ESCALOPE OF
SALMON WITH LEMON BUTTER
• MADAGASCAR PEPPER
STEAK • CHATEAUBRIAND
FOR TWO

RESERVE A WINDOW TABLE IF YOU CAN. FOR here, alongside the Bay of Fundy, views are of the world's largest tides urging nearer and nearer; and in summer, of harbour seals romping in the surf. ❦ Suited to 110 patrons, Turn of the Tide is a spacious, windowed room, soft with evening candlelight, appropriate music and comfortable surroundings. Within the birch and pine-trimmed restaurant, *The Captain's Table*, an enclosed room for 14, lends exclusivity to private functions. ❦ Restaurant Manager, Shirley Van Kralingen, provides well for her guests, smoothing the way toward menu presentations by Chef Mark J. Percival, veteran of a Michelin-rated kitchen in Oxford, England; and of Frankfurt's Culinary Olympics. Chef Percival favours regional bounty (fiddleheads, local berries, lamb) and insists on ocean-fresh fish and seafood. Beef is Alberta's top grade. The salmon, smoked at nearby Deer Island, is especially outstanding. A lean menu is planned for health-conscious diners who, like those who come to feast, will find the breads and pastries (baked on the premises) a great temptation. ❦ The polished service staff strives for excellence, taking pride in the kitchen's rating as one of worldwide Hilton's four finest. ❦ Wines from all major international regions are listed.

AVERAGE DINNER FOR TWO: $65
Does not include wine, tax and gratuity.

NORTHERN ITALIAN

DA MAURIZIO DINING ROOM

1496 LOWER WATER STREET
~ Within the Brewery Complex ~
HALIFAX, NOVA SCOTIA
(902) 423-0859

All major credit cards
Dinner Monday to Saturday

Proprietor
STEPHANIE
BERTOSSI

Proprietor & Chef
MAURIZIO
BERTOSSI

MENU HIGHLIGHTS

★★★★★

APPETIZERS
BRODETTO DI PECSE (SEAFOOD
SOUP) • WILD MUSHROOMS
SAUTÉED WITH WHITE WINE,
CREAM AND DEMIGLACE

MAIN COURSES
MELANZANE ALLA SAN
DANIELE • CARAMELLE
ALL'AGNELLO • SCALOPPINE
ALLA LOMBARDA • MARINATED
ROASTED DUCK • FRESH RABBIT
BRAISED WITH RED WINE AND
FRESH HERBS • FILETTO AL
FERRI (BEEF FILET) • SCAMPI IN
BUSERA • SALMONE ALLA BRACE
• CACIUCCO ALLA LIVORNESE

MAURIZIO BERTOSSI, A MAN OF FORMIDABLE talent, is the owner and inspiration behind this enormously personable restaurant. He began earning his culinary confidence as a boy in the northeast province of Italy, with his father, also a chef. Via Switzerland, the French and Italian Rivieras, Maurizio perfected his techniques, and for five years has been delighting Halifax with the sunny authentic tastes of northern Italian fare. ❦ Multiple courses from a lengthy, exciting menu promise a memorable dining experience in this accommodating room moody with Venetian masks, hand-blown grappa decanters, and soft lighting backgrounded often by the music of Italian opera. ❦ A large selection of homemade pastas are offered (ravioli with pumpkin and duck is outstanding) and antipasti showcase the sea. Main dishes of chicken, veal and seafood are lush with flavour and freshness. Grilled dishes are equally impressive. Order from the dessert menu with confidence. The ice creams and sorbets are homemade, tiramisu is perfection. ❦ A superb Italian collection balances the excellent wine list with representations from France, Australia and California.

AVERAGE DINNER FOR TWO: $60
Does not include wine, tax and gratuity

REGIONAL/CONTINENTAL

GRAND BANKER

1919 UPPER WATER STREET
~ Downtown, in the Sheraton Halifax Hotel ~
HALIFAX, NOVA SCOTIA
(902) 428-7852

General Manager
JIM MURAKI
Chef
DALE MCCARTHY

THE
MANAGEMENT TEAM

All major credit cards
Dinner Monday to Sunday • Lunch Monday to Friday
(Brunch Sunday)

MENU HIGHLIGHTS

★★★★★

APPETIZERS
STEAMED MUSSELS WITH TOMATO
BASIL BUTTER AND PARMESAN
TWISTS • SMOKED ATLANTIC
SALMON WITH WARM POTATO
PANCAKE, CAVIAR AND CRÈME
FRAÎCHE

MAIN COURSES
SCALLOPS, SHRIMP AND LOBSTER
SAUTÉED WITH PLUMS AND
TENNESSEE WHISKEY • ROAST
DUCKLING WITH APPLE GALETTE
AND BLACKBERRIES • GRILLED
RIB STEAK RUBBED WITH
ACADIAN SPICES, SERVED WITH
LOBSTER BROCHETTE

DESSERT
WARM SPICED BERRIES

ON THE WATERFRONT, NEXT TO THE FAMOUS Bluenose Tallship, is another Halifax attraction: The Grand Banker restaurant, located in the Sheraton Halifax Hotel and touted by *EnRoute Magazine* as "home of the best Sunday brunch in this city." ❦ Here, Executive Chef Dale McCarthy gives continental cuisine a regional twist, using the freshest of Nova Scotia's local bounty. Blackened Halibut, Digby Scallops, and Seafood Paella with Chicken, Red Peppers and Saffron Rice are big favourites. The innovative Grilled Rib Steak in Acadian Spices with Lobster Brochette is a definite must-try. Uncomplicated and à la carte, the menu offers a half-dozen meat and poultry selections, another half-dozen seafood choices and a smattering of pasta dishes. ❦ Restaurant General Manager Jim Muraki's youthful service team performs well and takes pride in the pleasure of its guests. ❦ The candlelit ambiance is subdued and cordial; nautical accents are tasteful and unobtrusive. ❦ An international list provides a balanced representation of French, Californian and Australian wines. ❦ *Also recommended is the fresh-grilled lobster at the hotel's Boardwalk Grill. Open summer season only, from June to September.*

AVERAGE DINNER FOR TWO: $50
Does not include wine, tax and gratuity.

CONTINENTAL

O'CARROLL'S

1860 UPPER WATER STREET
~ Downtown, one block from the waterfront ~
HALIFAX, NOVA SCOTIA
(902) 423-4405

All major credit cards
Dinner Monday to Sunday • Lunch Monday to Friday

Proprietor
JIM O'CARROLL

Chef
HUGH AUBRECHT

MENU HIGHLIGHTS

★★★★★

APPETIZERS
JUMBO SHRIMP COCKTAIL •
SEABRIGHT SMOKED SALMON
WITH A CRACKED PEPPER AND
MUSTARD DRESSING • DIGBY
SCALLOP MILLEFEUILLE

MAIN COURSES
FILLET OF HALIBUT EN
PAPILLOTES ON A JULIENNE OF
SWEET PEPPERS, ENHANCED WITH
CITRUS BUTTER • TENDER YOUNG
DUCK ROASTED AND PRESENTED
WITH GRILLED APPLE RINGS AND
CALVADOS CREAM • ATLANTIC
SALMON FLORENTINE • SUPREME
OF CHICKEN MARINATED IN
CANADIAN MAPLE SYRUP SERVED
ON APPLE PURÉE WITH AN
AMARETTO SAUCE

EXPERIENCED SAILORS KNOW A PORT'S BEST places are often found along the historic properties one block back from the waterfront. That's where to find the unique O'Carroll's Restaurant/Irish Pub. ❦ Donegal-born Jim O'Carroll is the heart of this place, always greeting new arrivals, spinning yarns, ensuring everyone has a good time. Transplanted 12 years ago from his own respected restaurant in Great Britain, Jim is accustomed to fine dining and fine wines. By culling the best from great restaurants in Europe and North America, and applying his experience and knowledge of the traditions and comfort zones of Halegonians, he has created magical results. ❦ The Irish Pub is to the right as you enter; the distinguished formal dining room, to your left. Tranquil and romantic at night, candlelit tables seat about 40. The uncomplicated menu's appealing variety of appetizers, main courses and desserts are cleverly handled. ❦ The gaiety of the adjoining pub/bar spills into the dining room, lending much to the atmosphere. Lyrical Irish melodies and spirited sea shanties enhance the relaxed experience. ❦ A good international wine list without pretension features some Nova Scotia wines. ❦ Later, feel free to drift into the Pub for a splendid Irish Coffee.

AVERAGE DINNER FOR TWO: $50
Does not include wine, tax and gratuity.

Proprietor & Host
DON CLINTON

Chef
NASIR

THE GRIFFON ROOM

200 POWNAL STREET
~ In The Dundee Arms Inn ~
CHARLOTTETOWN, PRINCE EDWARD ISLAND
(902) 892-2496

All major credit cards
Dinner Mon. to Sun. • Lunch Mon. to Sat.

MENU HIGHLIGHTS

★★★★★

APPETIZERS
STEAMED ISLAND BLUE
MUSSELS • MUSHROOM CAPS
STUFFED WITH PEI
ROCK CRAB

MAIN COURSES
LOBSTER PIE • LOCAL
ARCTIC CHAR • SEAFOOD
PALETTE • RACK OF LAMB

DESSERT
GRASSHOPPER PIE (GREEN
CRÈME DE MENTHE & CRÈME
DE CACAO, FROZEN, WITH
WHIPPING CREAM •
CHEESECAKE SELECTION

You may have read Griffon Room accolades in *EnRoute*, *Gourmet* or Japan's fashionable *Saison* magazines. The *Toronto Globe & Mail* says: "The (Dundee Arms) Inn's Griffon Room is acknowledged as one of Canada's finest restaurants." ❦ At home on a shady, residential Charlottetown street, this gently-restored Queen Anne mansion dating from almost a century ago is warmed with antique pine, Victorian mahogany, and period décor. ❦ Just opposite the Inn's Pub as you enter, the Griffon Room with its fireplace, exposed brick and eye-appealing artifacts, seats 45 in homespun comfort. ❦ Chef Nasir's eclectic menu is comprised of dishes Don Clinton (Innkeeper, Owner and Host) knows his guests like. Mushroom Caps Stuffed with PEI Rock Crab is a favourite starter to meals that range from Scallops Dundee to Indian Butter Chicken. Desserts are homemade. ❦ Refreshingly informal, the helpful service is professional, friendly, and altogether pleasing. ❦ The wine list is International and reasonable. ❦ On Saturdays, a very popular Brunch is offered. Veranda dining *al fresco* is a summer option.

AVERAGE DINNER FOR TWO: $45
Does not include wine, tax and gratuity.

THE CABOT CLUB

CAVENDISH SQUARE
~ In the Hotel Newfoundland ~
ST. JOHN'S, NEWFOUNDLAND
(709) 726-4980

Director of Food Service
Operations & Executive Chef
STEVE WATSON

Assistant Director of Food
Service Operations
& Maître d'
KEN RICHARDS

All major credit cards
Dinner Mon. to Sat. • Lunch Mon. to Fri.

MENU HIGHLIGHTS
★★★★★

APPETIZERS
CAESAR SALAD • COFFRET OF
SCALLOPS & SHRIMP

MAIN COURSES
FRESH ATLANTIC LOBSTER •
CATCH OF THE DAY • BEEF
PORTO • STEAK AU POIVRE
• RACK OF LAMB
• MEDALLIONS OF VEAL

DESSERTS
NEWFOUNDLAND
BERRY FLAN • WHITE
CHOCOLATE MOUSSE CAKE

THE VIEW ALONE IS ENOUGH TO ATTRACT guests to the relaxed elegance of The Cabot Club in the Hotel Newfoundland, but this exceptional dining room offers far more than stunning panoramas of Signal Hill and the glittering harbour from every table. ❦ By way of London's Mayfair, Executive Chef Steve Watson commands the kitchen with an enlightened touch and the eye of a perfectionist. Menus are purposely compact, featuring an appealing choice of starters; and about a dozen select entrées ranging from fresh fish, fowl and pasta to veal and chateaubriand. Cod, salmon and halibut are specialties; pan-fried, poached or steamed. Nothing is deep-fried. Enhancing the fine dining experience is the accommodating kitchen's credo; and the 28 cooks, 5 sous-chefs and pastry chef perform unfailingly. "If you don't find what you're looking for on the menu, please ask!" says Chef Watson. ❦ If you come in the spring, don't miss the fresh caribou. ❦ Service is formal, informed and very friendly under the expert direction of long-time Maître d', Ken Richards. ❦ French wines dominate an international list with selection of half-bottles offered.

AVERAGE DINNER FOR TWO: $60
Does not include wine, tax and gratuity.

★ ★ ★ ★ ★
WIN DINNER FOR TWO AT ANY RESTAURANT FEATURED IN THIS BOOK

★ ★ ★ ★ ★
(Transportation not included)

Simply provide us with your suggestions and comments before May 17, 1995

★ ★ ★ ★ ★

I would like to hear from you!

Firstly, did you find the inaugural edition of CANADA'S 100 BEST RESTAURANTS to be helpful? What improvements would you suggest?

Secondly, in a country as vast as Canada, there is no doubt that I have overlooked some very interesting "finds". New restaurants open every day. Old but great ones are sometimes forgotten. Great chefs sometimes move. For whatever reason, which restaurant(s) do you feel would be deserving of inclusion in the next edition of CANADA'S 100 BEST RESTAURANTS? (see over).

John R. McCann

John R. McCann
/PUBLISHER

COMMENTS AND SUGGESTIONS: _____

_____

_____

_____

_____

_____

_____

(See over)

SUGGESTED RESTAURANTS YOU WOULD RECOMMEND
TO BE FEATURED IN NEXT EDITION OF
"THE BEST RESTAURANTS OF CANADA"

RESTAURANT NAME: _____

CITY or TOWN: _____

(Based on 1-10, indicate your rating)

FOOD:_____ AMBIANCE:_____ SERVICE:_____ WINE LIST:_____

COMMENTS: _____

_____

_____

RESTAURANT NAME: _____

CITY or TOWN: _____

(Based on 1-10, indicate your rating)

FOOD:_____ AMBIANCE:_____ SERVICE:_____ WINE LIST:_____

COMMENTS: _____

_____

_____

Please mail to:

John R. McCann
PUBLISHER
CANADA'S 100 BEST RESTAURANTS
1155 Rene Levesque Blvd. W. Suite 2500
Montreal, Quebec, Canada H3B 2K4

Should I win, we would like to dine

at _____ in _____
      Restaurant Name   City or Town

Name: _____

Address: _____

City: _____

Province/State:_____ Postal Code/Zip:_____

ORDER YOUR COPY OF 100 BEST RESTAURANTS OF CANADA

❏ Yes! Please send me 100 BEST RESTAURANTS OF CANADA for only $14.95 plus $2.75 for postage & handling plus G.S.T., a total of 18.95 for EACH copy ordered.

❏ Best Offer. Save $20 I want four copies of 100 BEST RESTAURANTS OF CANADA and save $20. Regular price, incl. postage, handling & G.S.T. $75.80. Your price $55.80.

CALL (514) 871-9122
FAX (514) 875-8967

OR MAIL ORDER TO:

100 BEST RESTAURANTS OF CANADA
1155 Rene Levesque Blvd. W. Suite 2500
Montreal, Quebec
Canada   H3B 2K4

PLEASE MAIL THIS CARD IN AN ENVELOPE TO:

100 BEST RESTAURANTS OF CANADA
1155 Rene Levesque Blvd. W. Suite 2500
Montreal, Quebec
Canada   H3B 2K4

Name ———————————————————————————————————

Address ———————————————————————————————

City ————————— Prov./State ————————— ☐ ☐ ☐ ☐ ☐ ☐ ☐ ☐ ☐

☐ Cheque Enclosed   Postal Code/Zip

☐ Charge to: ☐ Visa ☐ MasterCard   ☐ American Express   ☐ Diners/En route

Card # Exp. ————————————————————————————

Signature ——————————————————————————————

Sorry, we do not bill, Please allow 3 weeks for delivery. Foreign orders, add $10.